For Edee—

Elderhostel 2009

A FUNNY THING HAPPENED ON THE ROAD TO SENILITY

Best Wishes

Carolyn Gray Thornton

A FUNNY THING HAPPENED ON THE ROAD TO SENILITY

I DISCOVERED THE JOY OF MIDDLE AGE-PLUS

Over 100 Humorous, Heart-Warming Stories of Middle Age-Plus

Carolyn Gray Thornton

Edited by
Ellen Gray Massey

Skyward Publishing, Inc.
Dallas, Texas
www.skywardpublishing.com

Copyright 2000 by Skyward Publishing, Inc.

Publisher: Skyward Publishing, Inc
17440 North Dallas Parkway
Suite 100
Dallas, Texas 75287
Phone/Fax (573) 717-1040
E-Mail: skyward@nsnw.net
Web Site: www.skywardpublishing.com

Library of Congress Cataloging-in-Publication Data

Thornton, Carolyn Gray, 1925-
A funny thing happened on the road to senility: I discovered the joy of middle age-plus / Carolyn Gray Thornton; edited by Ellen Gray Massey.
p. cm.
ISBN 1-881554-05-8
1. Middle age. 2. Aging. I. Title.
HQ1059.4.T53 2000
305.244--dc21

99-29788
CIP

Printed in the United States of America
Cover design by Dennis Riney
Illustrations by Jamie Holmes
Dennis Riney
Ann McCarthy

ATTENTION SCHOOLS AND CORPORATIONS

Skyward Publishing books are available at quantity discounts with bulk purchase for educational, business, or sales promotional use. For information write to:

Skyward Publishing, Inc.
Marketing
813 Michael Street
Kennett, Missouri 63857
(573) 717-1040
E-mail: skyward@nsnw.net

To my husband, Lester I. Thornton
for fifty-three years of love and
support as we became
Middle Age-Plus together

CONTENTS

3. MR. EDISON WOULD BE AMAZED

4. PHILOSOPHIES FROM WHERE I STAND

5. TIME OUT . . .

9. FAMILY IS FOREVER

10. THE RULES ARE CHANGING

ACKNOWLEDGMENTS

I would like to give special thanks to the following:

Jeff and Sandy Tweten, publishers of *N.E.W. Vernon County Record*, who took a chance by running my column after seeing only one sample of my writing and for their continuing support and encouragement.

Neal Swanson, publisher of Wainsley Press, Nevada, Missouri, who took the time to read my columns, made suggestions for marketing, and gave me encouragement to continue.

My siblings who gave me much material to write about as well as to continue to praise their little sister in her accomplishments.

My children and grandchildren who have supported my writing even when I was using them for subject matter.

My great-grandchildren for keeping me young enough to laugh about being middle age-plus.

My life-long boss, my childhood roommate sister, Ellen Gray Massey, who would not leave me alone until I did something about getting published and whose work as editor of this book meant hours of work, which took her away from her own writing.

And to the friends who read my columns weekly and encouraged me with comments and appreciation.

INTRODUCTION

I was one of those people who was never going to get old. I am the youngest of a large family, married to the youngest of a rather large family, so we have always been considered the young ones. Blessed with good health, I have sailed through all the pitfalls of the aging process such as menopause, emptynest syndrome, and the realization that I am a grandparent.

But a funny thing happened on the road to senility. I became a great-grandparent and discovered one day that I couldn't get out of a rocking chair with this new baby on my shoulder because there was nothing I could use to push myself out of the seat. I had seen others have this predicament and knew that it would never affect me that way. Obviously it did, and at the same time, I finally accepted the fact that if I wasn't old, I was at least past middle age.

Along with this acceptance, I began to see many good things about reaching this age. Today there is everything from twenty-seven cent soft drinks for seniors to numerous educational and vocational opportunities.

Since I had written newspaper columns in

earlier years called *Caught in the Middle* about being a middle-aged mother in a middle-sized town in the Midwest, I wanted to update this record by writing about my present stage. Therefore, I began writing weekly columns for our local newspaper, *The Vernon County Record*, about the pluses of being past middle age. *Middle Age-Plus* has chronicled my life for the past five years, recording the good and bad about changes in my family, my lifestyle, and most distressing, my body.

Since there is nothing we can do about many of the changes that come at this time of our lives, I enjoy finding the humor in many situations. Hopefully, this causes my readers to laugh at their own life changes along with me.

PROLOGUE

I love writing about the great things about becoming old, for the advantages are endless. There is so much knowledge in our heads that we can share with others. We don't have to study history. We lived it! I didn't live in the horse-and-buggy days, but my parents did, and since they shared their wisdom with me, I know many personal stories from that time. It seems that it wasn't as interesting to me when they were telling it as it is today. I probably didn't listen all that well, but I did listen enough to know that when I am ready to pass on my wisdom to my younger family members, it may be more interesting if it is written down.

I did live though the Depression. Also, I lived during World War II, the Korean War, Vietnam, and Desert Storm. I'm ready to limit my personal knowledge about wars. I'd rather remember the day when we had no U.S. involvement in wars.

I've gone from outhouses to saunas, from woodburning or kerosene cook stoves to microwaves, from fountain pens to computers, and sadly, from a care-free childhood to seeing my grandchildren and great-grandchildren being constantly warned about dangers.

When we are older, we realize it doesn't matter if our purse doesn't match our shoes or if the little ones don't always behave perfectly. We can relax about reading the small letters on the VCR, because we're too busy to have time to watch many movies anyway. It's not embarrassing to ask directions, because we have told many people where to go in earlier times. In short, it is a relaxed time of life with many good things to enjoy, and one thing I enjoy is writing.

Since a number of wonderful people who read my columns kept asking me to put together my work into a book, after five years, here it is. I hope others my age can enjoy a smile or a memory with me. And maybe those who are not old enough to quality will find reason to laugh with us and realize we had a lot of pluses to give our communities.

These essays were originally written for the residents of Vernon County, Missouri, which is a hundred miles south of Kansas City. The county seat, Nevada, has about 9,000 residents. What happened to me here, or in my childhood winter home in Washington, D.C., could have happened anywhere. Feel free to picture your own town or neighborhood as you read about mine.

So with all this wisdom and experience and knowledge I have stored up, why in the dickens can't I remember where I left my glasses?

Can This Be Me?

*You grow up the day you have your
first real laugh at yourself.*

Ethel Barrymore

I Hate Gravity

The further I progress on the road to middle age-plus, the angrier I am with Sir Isaac Newton. If he hadn't discovered the law of gravity, maybe my body would have a different shape today.

A quick look in the mirror shows the downward trend in every feature. The eyelids sometimes droop a little more than they used to. The corners of the mouth turn down instead of up, unless I am talking or smiling. I try to go around smiling when there is really nothing to smile about because I want to let my lips get a little altitude by being turned up for awhile.

The flesh from my arms has definitely felt the pull of gravity, and I won't even mention what is happening in other areas.

Our language about aging has also experienced old Isaac's law. We are *over the hill, winding down our lives,* or *slipping a little.*

If I weren't feeling so down, I would find out just how old Sir Newton was when he made this discovery. If legend has it right, he was sitting under an apple tree when it hit him (literally) that there was such a law. Since he was just lolling about that way, perhaps he, too, was middle age-plus with nothing better to do than ruin all of our faces for the next centuries!

Another thing that bothers me is that the law doesn't seem to have gender equality. The older male has not been treated the same by this discovery. Perhaps if a woman had time to be resting under the tree and had been hit with the apple, the law would have affected men more and women less. But then women have already had enough bad press concerning apples, so maybe it is just as well that Mrs. Newton wasn't the one who conceived the idea.

I wonder if it is a coincidence that *gravity* and *grave* come from the same root word? If Sir Isaac discovered this law, I imagine he could have named it anything he wanted to. The fact that he chose to make grave matters worse by giving it this somber name adds to my dislike of his old law.

If he had called the law by a cheerier name, maybe I would see the results in my body with more pleasure. But since I am a law-abiding citizen, I guess I will just lift up my spirits, smile a lot, and realize I don't care a fig about old Newton anyway.

My Colorless Eyebrows

I hardly ever think about eyebrows, but recently I was told that my eyebrows have very little color in them. In order to see well in the mirror, I need to have my glasses on, so my eyebrows are not noticeable because of the glasses' rims. If I don't have on my glasses, then I can't tell what they look like anyway, so I haven't worried about them.

But, like anything, once you notice it, you can't stop noticing it. Now I have become an eyebrow person. On the show *Suddenly Susan*, I noticed that Brooks Shields has very heavy eyebrows. They look good on her (what doesn't?) But I can remember when very stylish women plucked their eyebrows and replaced them with a thin, highly arched pencil line. I didn't think it looked very good then, but now when I think of it, I twinge at the needless pain of plucking each of those little hairs from that sensitive spot.

I suppose eyebrows have a needed function. My guess is that they are to shade our eyes somewhat and maybe keep foreign objects from our eyes. Since not many of us are beating our way through the brush each day, we aren't aware of what those little hairy arches might be needed for. But wouldn't our faces look funny without them?

I looked through all the family baby pictures I could find, and each of the babies in our families were born with eyebrows. However, some little bald babies don't get this facial ornament until later in their first year. They are so cute that this omission is not noticeable at all.

Now when we get older, as in all parts of our bodies, things begin to change. Men often develop quite bushy eyebrows. Remember Lionel Barrymore in the movies who used his bushy eyebrows eloquently to express emotion? Some men prefer to keep their eyebrows clipped to avoid that bushy look. Others let it be part of the overall appearance of the dignified older man.

Some people have experienced their eyebrows turning gray before their hair makes the change. And, in reverse, some with gray hair still have jet black eyebrows.

Since mine have been noticed as having little color, I don't know if that is a change with age or if it has always been that way. I am looking at my high school graduation picture, and although I am no Brooke Shields, I do seem to have sufficient eyebrows to punctuate my face. I didn't notice anyone at my wedding talking about colorless eyebrows, and my pictures there also show a prominent line of hair above my eyes.

Later pictures usually have been taken with me wearing glasses, so I don't know just when this drabness appeared. They aren't gray; they are just—blah! But a tint of red in the rims of my glasses has kept the world from noticing. In fact, it kept me from noticing until someone else told me about it.

Now as I sit here at my computer looking at all the family pictures on the wall in front of me, I see my mother in rimless glasses with well-defined eyebrows. Aunts, who were middle aged-plus when the picture was taken, also show ample foliage above their eyes. One brother was well-known for his expressive eyebrows, as he would emphasize statements by moving his eyebrows up or down. The brother whose complexion is the nearest to my coloring still seems to have no lack in this department, but he does have a more protruding brow than I do. That may disguise the lack of color somewhat if it is there.

I know there are eyebrow pencils still on the market, but since I have never used them in the past, I don't think I will start now. I guess a little drabness is nothing to raise your eyebrows about.

Praying Hands

I have learned to pray with my eyes closed. I am not trying to create a more spiritual mood. I am trying to keep from looking at the hands that are folded in my lap.

Nothing can take my mind off of a serious prayer more quickly than seeing all the checkered lines and bulging veins in my hands. Hands that are lying idle and being kept in a low position can show every sign of age. Loose skin, wrinkled paths going in every direction, prominent veins, liver spots, and cracked nails jump to my attention the minute I notice these usually busy appendages when they are lying idle.

I remember several years ago, when I was only middle aged, I was speaking to a club with my hands resting on the podium on top of my notes. I glanced down to keep my thoughts in order and noticed that my hands looked like I remembered my mother's hands. I thought, what are my mother's hands doing on the end of my arms? I later saw this quote in a publication, but at the time I thought it was an original shock reaction to a discovery. I was getting old, and my hands showed it. I lost the train of thought in my speech for a minute but assured myself that even if my hands were getting old, my mind was still young. I continued my presentation.

Since that time, I have become very aware of hands. They are the first harbinger of aging in most people. Men show this tendency, too, but not as quickly as women.

So what do we do? Several years ago a woman was not well dressed in public unless she wore gloves. I can see the benefits of that style now. I could focus on the threads in the gloves instead of the lines in my hands while I prayed if we still had this style. However, wearing gloves now would be more conspicuous and less comfortable than exposing my aging hands.

I thought about sitting on my hands or at least hiding them under the folds of my dress, but decided that would look rather odd, also. Then I decided that the value of these body parts was not in their appearance but in what they could do. I realized that these same hands are typing this essay. They made breakfast for my husband and me, washed dishes, made the bed, and held my great-grandchild as she celebrated her birthday.

That's more important than the signs of aging. But if any of you know of a good lotion I could try on my hands, I would be interested.

My Stylish Aunt

I had an aunt who was a very stylish and gracious person. But as a child, I was fascinated by the number of little red and brown nodules on her neck; one was even on her face. These little protrusions wiggled when she talked or when she turned her head. I became so fascinated by these moles that I didn't pay attention to what she said but just watched the movement of these little blemishes.

Everything about this aunt was first class. The home she and my uncle lived in was like a mansion to me. The house was filled with ornate furniture, which included an antique pump organ that we loved playing. Crystal chandeliers hung in the downstairs rooms. For that time, the house even had the unusual aspect of having a second full bathroom on the ground floor.

Her clothes were perfect for her slightly plump figure, and she had her hair done on a regular basis in a beauty shop. But what I remember, and what I noticed most, were these red and brown moles on her neck and face. At that time, I had no idea that such things could be removed easily by a doctor, but the number of them that she had would have made quite a procedure to do all at once.

When I was older, my father had some flat brown spots removed from his face. He said that he was not going to go into old age with brown spots all over his face. I had not noticed that he even had any spots, but then his did not wiggle or move. They were more like an enlarged freckle.

At different times as I was growing up, I noticed such growths on the necks and faces of various older friends and relatives. Of course, they did not concern me, for I was young, fair-skinned, and had only a few childhood freckles across my nose in the summer.

As I grew into adulthood, I had a small mole removed from my back by Dr. Pascoe because my clothing irritated it. Since he said this could possibly lead to something more serious, I had it removed.

For many years I did not notice anything else changing about my skin color or texture. But then middle age-plus set in. I could now have a standing appointment with a surgeon and not keep ahead of all the beauty spots that are appearing. Some I have had removed because of a potential danger or because of a very conspicuous location. But most of them abide with me still.

This morning I was washing my teeth and looking into the bathroom mirror. (I still say bathroom mirrors should be abolished when one passes middle age.) As I was vigorously brushing my teeth, I suddenly noticed the little red and brown protrusions on my neck were also vigorously bobbing up and down. Forgive me, Aunt Lil. I am being punished for the attention I gave to the skin on your poor neck and face when everything else about you was so perfect. Now I have the same problem.

I wonder how many children have been mesmerized by the actions on my neck? I knew the growths were there, of course, but until this morning I had not noticed their dance routines. Aunt Lil was not a blood relative but was the wife of my father's brother; therefore, the condition couldn't be inherited except as an aspect of aging.

Let's make a pact together. If you are over, say, sixty and we meet, I will not look at the skin on your neck and face if you will not look at mine. Of course, if you happen to sit in front of me at church and have a mark on the back of your neck, I could hardly keep from noticing. But I will not let it hypnotize me into seeing nothing else. Unless it wiggles!

In the meantime, I am going to wear a lot of turtleneck shirts.

I Don't Like the Term "Elderly"

Who is elderly? I was at a meeting recently when a friend was explaining the benefits of some modern technology for the elderly. I couldn't see why she was talking about this to ME. I may be middle age-plus, but I am not elderly! Another friend, who is in my age group, was very upset when a fender-bender accident she was in described her in the newspaper as a seventy-year-old elderly woman. She didn't mind that the report told her age, but she balked at being called elderly.

At our age, we can relax about reading the small letters on the VCR because we're too busy to have time to watch many movies anyway. It's not embarrassing to ask directions, because we have told many people where to go in earlier times! In short, it is a relaxed time of life with many good things to enjoy.

Some describe us as Senior Citizens. Others just use the term Seniors. To some we are Golden Agers, but to most we are just plain *old*. But when one of us is asked about the terms, we each have our own definitions about our age. I personally don't consider myself old. Sure, I am getting old, but so is every person reading this article. I don't object to the term Senior, or Senior Citizen, especially when it means I get a discount on my hamburger. It brings back the school day memories of looking up to the Seniors. They were the ones who had it made. They had successfully completed most of the course and were about to go on to greater things. We envied them.

Being a Senior in life carries the same idea. We have almost completed the course, yet we are not eager to go on to other things. We'd prefer to remain in the school of life for many more years. I suppose Seniors can be kept back and keep repeating that graduating year. But in time that could get boring.

Golden Ager has a nice ring, but for some the age is anything but golden. Hopefully, most of us have many golden moments in any age. As a whole, the golden times are just as numerous in any stage of life.

Let's see, what does that leave? Old. I see old people around town, but they are usually ones I don't know very well. When I think of friends my age or those a little older, I still don't think of the word old. Perhaps I realize they have a few years on me, but that doesn't make them old.

I don't intend to ever become elderly. I will someday admit to being old (maybe). But being elderly has a negative connotation that I don't like.

My unabridged dictionary defines "elderly" as rather advanced in years, past middle age, old-fashioned, out of date, outmoded, relating to one who is past the prime of life. So of the six definitions, I see myself in only one and that isn't enough to count!

I hope to continue being middle age-plus for a good many years, but I do not plan to answer to the name of elderly.

What I'd Never Do

There were several things that I promised myself that I would never do when I got older. I was never going to turn my head back like I was looking at the stars when I read the newspaper or looked at a notice on the bulletin board.

I did not think I would ever push myself up from a chair or from a kneeling position instead of letting my legs lift me up. I was not going to get thick through the middle so that my waist line just sorta blended into my hips. I felt secure that the back of my upper arms would remain firm and not sway in the breeze when I waved my arms. I knew that my profile would show no signs of a double chin nor would I get the little deposit of fat on each side of my chin.

Certainly, I would avoid the stern look that many older persons have when they're not intending to be all that serious. And I wouldn't have thinning or graying hair. Things of that nature happened to other aging folks. I was going to avoid them. Because I am the youngest in my family, there was no way I could assume the telltale signs my siblings began to show. People said I didn't look my age, and I believed them.

I am writing this on a computer screen that is a little above eye level. My neck is getting tender from throwing my head back so that I can read the words on the screen. I noticed the same thing last night when I was reading the paper.

I rearranged my closet today. Some clothes I decided to give away because they were a little too snug or should I say downright tight at the waist. Could some of the children use them?

While kneeling to sort the shoes at the bottom of the closet, I had a little problem trying to rise with old shoes in my hands. A little push on the floor helped me get up more easily. While trying on some of the clothes to see how they now fit, I got a good look at my arms. They look great from the elbows to the hands, anyway.

Later while driving to town, I caught a glimpse of myself in the outside rear view mirror. I was startled. Was that a turned-down mouth between two little paunches of fat by my chin. I stopped the car and pulled down the visor to look in the vanity mirror. I decided that vanity wasn't the name my mirror should have--reality is more like it. I reassured myself that my hair is not VERY gray and still covers all of my head.

Being on the road to middle age-plus can be a shock at times. I don't feel like I'm old. Inside I really feel like a much younger person. If I stay away from mirrors, wear long sleeves, and smile a lot, maybe I can live up to the promise I made when really young.

Why Is It That...?

Some of the things about getting old puzzle me. It seems there is an ironic coincidence in the timing of events and changes that come our way.

For instance, why is it that when loss of hair in desired spots begins, an abundance of hair suddenly appears in spots like ears and noses of men and upper lips and chins of women? If the body can still produce all that hair, why not leave it on the top of the head?

Or why is it that when a couple finally has enough leisure time to sit down and have a nice conversation over a meal or in the porch swing, the main topic of conversation is trying to recall the names of past friends, or even present friends, we saw today but weren't sure of the names.

Speaking of names, why is it that when we begin to get interested in our genealogy and want to know our ancestry, all the folks who could have easily filled us in have gone to join their ancestors?

Also I wonder why when we now have time and a little money to travel, we find that we really prefer staying home where we are more comfortable? It's great to get away for a few days, but then home begins to look very good so that trip plans get edited severely.

And as badly as we wanted to see our families and spend quality time with the grandchildren or great-grandchildren, why is it that we are somewhat relieved when everyone goes home, and we have the house back to ourselves again? Another thing. Why is it that now, when I have time to do a better job of housekeeping and tidying up the place, the floor has suddenly become so much lower and the ceiling higher when I am cleaning or picking things up?

Then there's the irritation that now we have enough money to buy a few more exotic foods to eat, but our waistlines or digestive systems forbid it.

When watching television with our nice new larger screen, why do we find we now have trouble hearing all the mumbled words that explain the plot?

Why now, when I have the time to swim, canoe, or ice skate on our front lawn pond, do I find that it just seems like too much trouble? I would rather just watch the waterfowl or other people enjoy the water.

Yes, it seems that timing is very important and these ironies of possibilities and time to carry them out don't always coincide. When middle age-plus, there are other possibilities that seem pretty great. The privilege of walking, seeing, hearing, and even breathing remains gifts, even in somewhat impaired states. As long as today exists, life is full of new adventures that fit our changing needs.

Would anyone like to join me in eating a bowl of popcorn seated in a lounge chair?

I Passed for Fifty!

Yesterday I was mistaken for someone who was celebrating her fiftieth birthday. Now not even on my better days do I feel that I could pass for a fifty-year-old woman. If so, I'd be writing this column under false pretenses. I consider fifty as middle age, not middle age-plus.

I can't help admitting, however, that it really gave me a good feeling for awhile to even consider that I looked that young.

Then I came home and later took a bath. I think big mirrors and good lighting should be outlawed in the bathroom of anyone over sixty. Here I was, basking in the glow of the unintended compliment, and then I had to see myself clearly in that (deleted) mirror.

We've been told about the dangers that the sun can do by too much exposure. It will dry out your skin and make wrinkles appear as you age. What I was looking at had rarely seen the sun. But the wrinkles are certainly there. Well, I can't really call them wrinkles. They look more like a contour map of the land, like you see in a good atlas or on a weather map on television. You know, the ones that show the mountainous areas and little streams and rivers running every which way between the hills.

My body seems to have very few smooth plains in this contour map but many, many lines for streams and rivers.

Some of the lines disappeared as I turned myself in different directions to make the skin tighter, but it would be very awkward to walk around in those positions.

I consoled myself that only someone who really, really loved me (barring emergency personnel) will ever see this portion of my anatomy.

I realized that the woman who had thought I was only fifty had seen me wearing long sleeves, slacks, and a fresh hairdo. It is hard to take a bath while wearing long sleeves and slacks, with or without a fresh hairdo. Since it is also hard to take a bath in the dark, I guess I will have to face up to myself at least daily as someone who does look her age.

But maybe once in a while I will fool someone else again and for a few minutes feel that I really do look as young as I feel. Hey, inside I really am only fifty and that is not only on my better days!

Japanese Eye Charts

Have you ever noticed the different way people hold their hymn books at church? Some hold them right in front of their faces, and others hold them out at arms' length. The most common position seems to be holding the book about chest level at the end of a bent arm.

When I recently had my eyes tested, Dr. Hatch told me that he could pretty well guess people's age by the way they hold a hymnal or any reading material. No one has to try to guess my age, so I will admit that I no longer like to share a hymn book because another person's comfortable position makes it hard for me to read. If I place it where I can see it, then it isn't right for my neighbor.

Thankfully, I know most of the words well enough to fake it if I can't read every line, but just as sure as I am sharing a book with a short person, the minister will choose a hymn that is unfamiliar. It is an asset to the congregation when I can't read the words because then maybe I won't sing, and people will be spared hearing my voice. But my voice singing the *wrong* words is even worse.

The older people who have had cataract surgery are often gaily singing away with their books held any which way because they now have excellent vision again. But I am in that awkward state—not far enough along to need surgery but far enough along to need all the help I can get when reading.

I heard on a news show that people at a certain age (I don't remember what the age was) need eight times more light than younger people. Maybe that is why we have chosen not to put any coverings over our windows because we love to have the rooms light and airy. I can read in bed with only a small bedside lamp, but I often fall asleep more quickly than if I am in a well-lit room.

I am eager to see how I will do with my new glasses. It might not have been a really accurate testing because many of the eye charts I was instructed to read were written in Japanese. When Dr. Hatch magnified them, they turned into English letters, but I think he had a switch somewhere that he could press to make the change.

Also those little spokes that are sometimes dark and sometimes lighter kept changing on me. It's hard to tell which is darker than another when they keep switching. I have the same trouble when I am ironing a striped or dotted garment. I have solved that fairly well by not ironing most things.

I like to enjoy the darkness of a night without any lights. There is quite a bit of light in nature's nights. The stars, moon, and distant horizons all have areas of light that are beautiful to watch. It is not so beautiful when I am driving through periodic areas of artificial light, oncoming headlights, and neon signs blinking on and off. Add a little rain on the windshield, and I am a lost cause. However, I love to drive at night out on the open road where there are very few other cars to have headlights facing me. Divided highways are another big help, since the headlights are not right in my face.

So in my aging process I could get along fine if it weren't for other people. If I could hold my own book, adjust my own light, keep everyone else off the road at night, my eyesight would be no problem. But it might get a little lonely. And since I don't qualify for a seeing eye dog for company yet, I guess I will have to adjust to my problem.

If you sit next to me in church, just hand me a hymnal, and we will be friends for life!

Hear! Hear!

It's funny how life teaches you humbling lessons. I recently experienced what I hope is a temporary condition with my ears. Fluid has collected behind my eardrums. My friends all know by now that I have water on the brain, but this is somewhat different. It is similar to the feeling in your ears when you have just landed from an airplane. It sounds as though you are inside a glass bottle and all other sounds are coming from outside this bottle. That is all sounds except the sounds in your own head such as swallowing, chewing, and your own voice. These sounds come on with amplification.

When I was at a dinner party the other night, I had to leave some of my crackers on the plate beside my soup bowl because the sound inside my head from eating the crackers was so loud that I couldn't hear even a tiny portion of the conversation around me. I smiled and nodded my head as friends spoke to me. I hope that they weren't telling me dire news.

Now I really understand what those who have hearing losses are going through. After awhile, you tire of asking people to repeat, and, as important, after awhile, other people get tired of having to repeat. You do one of two things. You guess at what was said and risk miscommunications, or you just withdraw from conversations and become a loner. If no one is around to talk to you, then you don't have trouble hearing them!

It becomes easier to stay home from social events or even from going shopping or doing errands when the pressure to hear is greater than the pleasure of social interaction. It is also more pleasant to withdraw to the television in the bedroom where you can turn the volume high rather than watch with your family and miss all meaning because you can't hear.

Those with chronic hearing loss can usually get relief with the great new hearing aids. Much of what I am temporarily experiencing is lessened for them.

There are even new surgical procedures that do wonders for the hearing impaired, but often tensions develop in a gray period in between normal hearing and admitting the need for some outside help.

Family members can no longer expect you to hear them when they are talking to you from another room or while walking away from you. People who talk to you on the telephone must realize that when you can't actually see the person, it is even harder to hear.

Then there is a problem with those who talk fast, who drop their voice at important times, or talk through partially closed lips. All these circumstances make it doubly hard for those who don't hear well.

All of these things are lessons that I should have learned myself years ago when I was with others who had some hearing loss. But we seem to develop a feeling of superiority over those with some disabilities without realizing what we are doing. When it is obvious to us what someone else is saying, we tend to forget that others may not hear. When we hear a bird call, or the clock strike, it doesn't occur to us that maybe everyone didn't hear it, too.

I remember the frustration I felt when trying to carry on a conversation with loved ones who weren't hearing well. Now I realize the much greater frustration that a loved one must have been experiencing in the same conversation, for I know that it is as physically tiring to strain for sounds as it is to strain for other reasons.

When I finish the round of medication that is supposed to bring me out of my sound bottle, I plan to be more understanding of the physical problems of others. I will watch for signs that show a possible problem and do what I can to help the situation. I will try to remember what it was like in this twilight zone of muffled sounds.

Do you hear what I am saying?

Not a Knot

When I was a little girl, I used to worry about how I would wear my hair when I got old. Every older woman that I knew then (and that even included the really old ones in their fifties) wore her hair in a knot either at the back of her head or in a looser twirled knot on top of her head. My mother had her knot at the nape of her neck. I thought the waves she put into her hair before it got into the knot looked much better than those neighbors who pulled their hair straight back into the knot. In later years, my mother wore a braid around her hair. I liked that much better.

But back to my worries. I'd never wanted a knot at the back of my head. It bothered me to even think about it. My Buster Brown haircut suited me just fine, but I knew then that I couldn't wear it that way when I got older.

I watched for some different style on my mother's friends and finally decided if I had to have some sort of knot, I preferred the French knot that some ladies at church wore.

Now that I am middle age-plus, and still wear my hair about the same way I have worn it since high school, I have to laugh at my childhood worries. As I look at other women, I see very few who have any knot at all. Quite a few sport the very same Buster Brown haircut that I was wearing when I became concerned about my old age style.

One of the great things about today is that almost anything goes in style of dress, hair, or shoes. The women who are most apt to have their hair pulled straight back into a knot are not the older women but the young ones with perfect features and complexions. We older women feel more comfortable with a little softness and curl to detract from our aging faces.

I didn't worry about hair color when I was young because I was not aware of anyone dyeing hair. Today you can see almost any color of hair (even blue), but I prefer the colors that nature has given us. The softness of graying hair or the purity of snow white hair frames our older faces in a more flattering way than any dye job can.

When I look at pictures of my mother with the hairstyles of the past, I don't know why I was so worried. She looks very pretty, and the style is becoming to her. But I am still glad that I don't have to wear mine that way.

Now my only concern is that I won't keep enough hair to worry about how I will wear it.

Fears and Phobias

When you reach middle age-plus, you are scared of different things than when you were young. However, there are some things that I have always been afraid of. My mother passed on her great fear of snakes to me. Intellectually I know most snakes are nothing to fear, yet intellect and fear do not always go hand in hand. I can see a snake in a field and not shiver, but if I am walking in the field and suddenly see one by my feet, I not only shiver, but I jump and yell. However, I think that I would be just as upset if I knew in advance that a snake was going to cross my path.

A recent story on television about a city apartment dweller who went into her bathroom to find a very long python coming out of her toilet was enough to make me turn on the light at every midnight trip to the bathroom.

I first thought this was one of the new urban folk tales that has developed. But they showed a tape of the reptile still coming from the toilet bowl.

That was more proof than I really wanted to see.

Another thing that I have always been afraid of is getting sick in public. I suppose when I was very young that wasn't a worry, but I can remember school days when I almost made myself sick thinking about how horrible it would be not to be able to leave the room if I were sick. This has translated in later life as wanting a seat near the aisle at church or in a theater. I have never disgraced myself so far, but I have great sympathy for the poor man in the Imodium AD commercials who is facing the long flight of stairs in a stadium as he is working his way to the restroom.

But now a whole different set of fears has hit me. I'm afraid that I will run into a very good friend and not be able to come up with her name. For this reason, I fear introductions. I can start out making an introduction and lose the name of one of my friends right in the middle of the process. Sometimes I get by with something like "I want you two good friends to meet each other," and hope that they will then supply their own names.

I also fear forgetting where I left my car in a parking lot. That's not too bad when I'm alone, for I can usually find it fairly soon. But when a nice young helper is following me with my groceries, it's downright embarrassing to wander over the lot. It's especially bad if the lot is nearly empty. That happened when I was driving our new pickup and forgot I wasn't in our car. Since the new pickup hadn't been clearly impressed in my memory bank, I walked by without realizing this was the vehicle I had been searching for.

Somehow in my adult years I have developed a strong dislike, if not a real phobia, about driving across narrow, high bridges that have a lot of overhead stucture that seems to entrap me. The worst one of this type is across the Missouri River at Boonville, Missouri, on old U.S. Highway 40. This bridge has a chain link bottom that vibrates the car as you drive over it, and you can see through it to the river far below. The purpose of this type of structure is to prevent the whole bridge from giving way during a flood. What it has accomplished for me is a fear reaction when I see a similar bridge on the road ahead.

When I travel with my sister Ellen, we have a pact. She will drive over this type of bridge if I will drive in the cities. Sometimes it is impossible to stop to change drivers in time. And though I do manage to stay on course, my knuckles are usually white when I finally get across.

I just had a thought. Do you suppose this is some innate fear of crossing the River Jordan? If so, I hope when the time comes, I won't be driving!

Probably the worst fear I have now is the fear of mirrors. I can be having a great time relaxing at home, working with a group of friends, enjoying an outing, or attending a meeting when I happen to catch a reflection of myself in a nearby mirror. No matter how many times a day I use a mirror for grooming, I still get a shock when I accidentally see my reflection. I don't know who that old woman in the mirror is because the younger one inside me is not that old! She knows she is middle age-plus, but that reflection sometimes makes her look so OLD.

Maybe if I go by myself, park my car in an unforgettable spot, walk across a bridge high enough to keep me from seeing any snakes, but not high enough to make my stomach get upset, and avoid looking at any reflective materials, I can avoid my fears.

But I wouldn't have any fun! So I guess I'll go back to the car, find some friends to join me, and take my chances on running into any frightening things as I continue to enjoy my journey of life.

Maybe It Will Go Away

Who do you see when you look into a mirror? I often get startled when I glance in a mirror and see one of my aunts, my mother, or maybe an older sister. I would be pleased to think I really did look like any of these people, but what startles me is that I look old enough to look like them.

Since Lester and I are each the youngest in our families, we have always been considered young by our siblings. At one time that was a burden. We were too young to join in certain family outings or activities. We were too young to understand, too young to be trusted with a job, or too young to read that book or see that movie.

Then came the years when it was an advantage to be the youngest. We were not only included in all the activities and conversations, we often were the leaders.

Now comes the time when it is sad to be the youngest because we have to face the aging of our siblings and share with nieces and nephews some responsibility for solutions for care of these relatives who were our childhood heroes. Then when I look into the mirror and see some of these older loved ones looking back at me, I realize that not only are we not the young ones anymore, but we are the older generation.

What do we do about it?

There really is nothing we can do to change the facts, but we can face the reality and make plans.

Already I have planned that I will never need to go to a nursing home. I plan to remain hale and hearty up to the last moment and not need any special care.

I have also planned that I will not look a whole lot older than I do now. Maybe a wrinkle or two here or there, or a few more gray hairs, but nothing really drastic.

Other plans include continuing to be active in organizations that I enjoy and being a valuable member of each right up to the end. I will perhaps step down some from leadership, but everyone will depend on me for advice and opinions.

My driving will remain safe and certain while I am getting myself from home to these many activities. My family will never worry about my safety as I will give them no reason to be concerned.

My hands, head, or other extremities will not shake, my vision will remain keen, and my voice will not weaken.

Best of all, my memory will not fade and even names will not escape my keen mind.

Yes, I have learned from the experiences of my elders and made these plans for myself. I'm ignoring the tremor I see when holding my hymnal in front of me for several minutes. I don't see the sagging skin on my arms when they are in certain positions.

I don't see these things because they are not in my plans. Like most of those who have gone before me, I plan to avoid all the problems of becoming older. And one way to carry out my plans is to be blind to the signs that I see each day. If I don't dwell on these changes, maybe they will go away. Sometimes when the children were little, if they were fussing and I ignored them long enough, the problem would go away.

Now age and I are fussing, and I plan to ignore the dispute until maybe it will go away. I don't plan to be a problem to my children because these ignored symptoms will go away. Good planning will insure that my old age will be a blessing to everyone involved.

There is a poem by the Scottish poet, Robert Burns, that states, "The best-laid schemes o' mice an' men gang aft agley." (go often astray). You don't think that could happen to me, do you?

Just in case I probably should avoid that mirror.

Other People Look So Old!

Have you noticed how old other people look these days? When I meet a female friend I haven't seen for awhile, I can't get over how old she looks. Of course, we each go through the pleasant lies about how good each of us looks, but I still marvel at how quickly she has aged.

Why it wasn't but five, no maybe ten, years ago that we were taking our little grandchildren roller skating together. Oh, oh, I guess it was longer ago than that since those little grandchildren now have school age children of their own. But it doesn't seem that long ago. Now she has trouble getting up from a chair.

I think I have matured easily with very little outward signs of my actual age. After all, I am younger than all of my family, and I haven't completely retired yet. The fact that yesterday I had trouble getting out of the back seat of a two door car wasn't really a sign of any deterioration. They just don't design cars the right way anymore.

I did notice just a bit of gray in my hair today when the light hit it just right, but many people gray prematurely. I have a niece who is completely gray, and she is twenty-five years younger than I am.

So the gray hairs don't really worry me.

We became great-grandparents for the fourth time this week with the birth of little Jerron Trey Thornton. Having another great grandchild is a thrill and doesn't make me feel any older.

What makes me feel older is that my son is three times a grandfather. It was just a few years ago that he graduated from high school.

Recently, I was visiting a woman who doesn't seem much younger than I am. I mentioned how excited I was when John Glenn took his first orbit in space. She confessed that she was too young to remember the event.

I was pregnant with my fourth child at the time! So I guess I am a little older than she.

There is much excitement on the airways about new releases of *The Wizard of Oz.* It was perfectly good when it was first put out a few years ago. I begin wondering why they had to enhance it. I was in junior high when I first saw the show in the theater and still vividly remember the lions and tigers and bears, oh my!

Since I graduated from junior high in 1940, I realize it was a ways back. I can still sing all the songs or at least know the words. I never could really sing them if anyone was listening to me and wanted to know the tune.

I was interrupted while writing this essay by our neighbor coming to the door. I remember this man's father when he was too young to go to school, and now he had his fourth grandchild this week and has another on the way. I even remember his grandfather and great-grandfather, so I have known six generations of this family. Maybe that does make me sort of old.

If all my friends are beginning to look old to me, maybe I look that way to them, also. If I really look in the mirror, I have to agree it is true. Maybe I ought to call the doctor for a check-up. When you feel young, even if you are middle age-plus, it's good to take care of yourself.

And I don't want to hear what my friends say about me after we meet again after time has passed. I might have to face my real age.

What Is Middle Age-Plus?

I have decided that it is time to set some definitions on just who is middle age-plus. Middle age is supposed to be the period when your life is approximately half over.

But most people don't admit to being middle aged until they are over fifty, and there aren't that many one-hundred-year-old people running around (Actually, there are probably *very few* running around. Maybe some are walking around slowly.) But what is middle age-plus?

The following may help you decide who can claim this title.

You are middle age-plus if you refer to the appliance that keeps your food cold as an *icebox*.

You are middle age-plus if you know all the words to "Amy Buddy."

You qualify if you don't feel the need to wash your hair every day.

Also if you call "Bibbers" "overalls," you probably can join the group.

When you serve breaded tomatoes with your meals occasionally, you are middle age-plus. And if you have no idea what your cholesterol count is, you can be counted (but, maybe not for long).

If you remember when "having a dish in the lawn" meant you had a pet dog who needed water, you are one of us.

If you start many sentences with "When I was your age...", you are a charter member of the group.

You are middle age-plus if you have enough sense to take a coat along in the car because the weather can change suddenly in March even if it is nice right now or if you keep reminding others to do the same.

When giving directions, if you refer to turns as the "old Jones Place" or "three miles past the brickyard hill", then you probably are middle age-plus.

Those of us who realize that the hardest part of being a parent begins when the child becomes an adult are definitely ready to be called middle age-plus.

And those who love to have grandchildren or great-grandchildren visit, but *really* love it when they go home, have reached that age.

There are those who honestly don't feel they are old enough to be called middle age-plus but whose birthday candles set off the smoke alarm. They are cherished members of our thriving group.

Another sign is you are relieved or even down-right happy when an event you were planning to attend has been called off, and you get to stay home. This is especially true for meetings, but it is also the case for social events. The lounge chair and the television seem pretty good when you thought that you would be gone from them for awhile.

Another sign is looking at the number of pages

in a book or an article before selecting it to read. You choose the short ones first, putting the longer ones back until you have a little more free time.

Housekeeping duties don't seem as important these days. Since most of your friends are middle age-plus too, they probably aren't going to drop by very often, and if they do, their eyesight won't let them see the dust that probably is there. You don't see any, do you?

Cooking from scratch is no longer a point of pride. Frozen pie crusts ready for a can of prepared fruit does just fine, if you even bother to do that much. After all, the bakeries have to make a profit!

In spite of a closet full of clothes, it is easier to put on the ones you just wore the other day. You know everything is in repair on them, and if you dig deeper in your closet, no telling what you may find that needs mending or new buttons.

If all the tellers at the bank, the clerks in the stores, and even the doctors and nurses in the clinics look like they are just kids, you have reached the middle age-plus plateau with the rest of us.

But this age is a pretty nice place to be. After all, if we can be a little more laid back and enjoy taking the easier path, we can still remember all those steeper, rocky roads we traveled for so many years. This is really the time when you feel good enough for most things, but you don't really care if you do them or not. I don't think I would want to go back to another age right now. I might be expected to find something useful to do whenever an event has been called off.

2

Saran Wrap
and Panty Hose

*I've learned that you can tell a lot about
a person by the way he handles these three
things: a rainy day, lost luggage, and
tangled Christmas tree lights.*

M. Achuff

Drop the Handkerchief

Are any of you women readers carrying a handkerchief?

I have a packet of Kleenex tissues in my purse and pockets full of folded tissues in whatever I wear, but I don't think I have a single cloth handkerchief except in my dresser drawer. Most of those were given to my mother years ago, and I couldn't bear to part with them.

As a child, I had many uses for handkerchiefs, and I usually had one somewhere in my clothes. While at Sunday school, my pennies for the offering were tied into a knot in the corner of the hankie.

Likewise, my milk money for school was safely tied into a hankie, which was pinned to my dress or inside a pocket.

My mother used a handkerchief corner for spit baths on the way to Sunday School when she noticed dirt behind my ear or jelly left on my chin. Though I hated that process, I found myself repeating it with my children.

Now upon noticing a smudge on a grandchild or great-grandchild, I whisk out my packet of

Handi-Wipes for a cleanliness S.O.S. while remaining antiseptic.

I often made a makeshift hat from a large handkerchief by tying knots in each of the four corners. This made a beret-type headgear that I wore for make-believe games.

And, of course, it was very helpful to have a handkerchief so I could be the first one to be "it" in the game of Drop the Handkerchief. Although I never used my hankie as a flirtation device, according to movies and books, accidentally dropping a hankie was a tried and true attention-getter.

During the Sunday sermon, while the minister told of animal sacrifices in Biblical times, I thought of the mess that would be for someone to clean up. Then, sacrilegiously, I thought of the congregation being splattered with blood and wondered what the parents in those days did. Did they use a corner of a robe or toga moistened from their mouths to clean off the child? Or do you think they carried something similar to our handkerchiefs?

Reassuringly, I felt inside my purse for the tiny packets of Handi-Wipes and Kleenex. Even though I don't expect to be splattered with blood, my instincts tell me to be prepared for a quick clean-up. I don't want another middle age-plus person behind me spotting a blemish. If that happened, I might need a quick spit bath again.

Remember Leg Make-Up?

The invention of panty hose has been a big advance for womankind. When I think back to some of the methods of wearing stockings in the past, I give thanks to the bright person who dreamed up this idea.

Someday I will do some research into this important subject, but my guess is that the decline of corsets and girdles brought on the need for another way to keep stockings up. Those garments of torture—namely corsets and girdles—did have contraptions on the bottom to fasten stockings. Any woman who escaped that underwear armor used garter belts. I still see them in the catalogs but have absolutely no interest in buying one again.

I remember my older sisters wearing hose rolled just below or above the knee. Fancy garters used for holding up stocking were reserved for weddings or other fancy events. At that time, I wore knee socks and didn't understand the problem, though I remember the discussions my sisters had with mother about the propriety of wearing rolled hose *below* the knees. During the war (if you are middle age-plus, you don't need to describe which war), material for stockings was scarce, since silk stockings came from our enemy, Japan. We wore some awful-looking rayon stockings, went bare-legged, or wore leg make-up.

One memorable hot August day during the war, my best friend and I went to Olathe, Kansas, where there was a Naval training station. Since we wanted to look our best for the sailors we spent the day with, we each rubbed on flesh colored leg make-up to go with our white dresses and heels.

When the sailors joined us in our small coupe, my friend and I took turns sitting on the lap of one of the sailors. We had a lovely time riding to the park, getting cokes, and listening to the car radio.

When it was time for the men to return to base and us to return home, we were dismayed. The leg make-up had rubbed from our hot, sweaty legs onto the dress whites of the two sailors. As they walked away from the car, we saw long tan streaks down the sparkling white pant legs.

We, in turn, had long smeared streaks in our carefully prepared leg make-up. We wondered why we never heard from those men after that!

I never used leg make-up again.

By the '60s, slacks were permissible almost anywhere, and we had started wearing panty hose to cover our legs. Still, wearing panty hose had problems, too. The early ones had seams up the back similar to ordinary stockings. Trying to keep the seams straight, along with the gyrations of putting on the panty part of the hose, became quite a challenge. The seams twisted and twisted again, making any leg watcher get dizzy. I was glad when seamless ones came out.

I need tall sizes in panty hose. Since I am no longer skinny, or even thin, I must be careful that the tall size also allows for an ample rear. Nothing is more disconcerting than rising to sing the closing hymn in church than to discover that your panty hose has slipped below the panty level. You walk out with the whole thing beginning to tumble down to your knees.

Careful shopping and dressing helps us avoid most of the pitfalls of panty hose. But I will continue to praise the concept until something better comes along.

My New
Compartmentalized Purse

I bought a new purse today and moved into it tonight. Though I found only fifteen things in my old purse that didn't need to be put into the new one, I found much more that did need to stay with me.

I have never been one to have a purse for every outfit. That meant changing the contents from one to another frequently. I usually buy one big black purse to carry on all occasions, except maybe when I use a fanny pack while on a walk or at a picnic.

The lining in my old purse ripped, and I kept losing my car keys in the far reaches of my purse as they slipped through the lining.

But what really made me break down and get a new purse was that the handles on the old one were worn out. I was afraid I would lose the whole thing some day.

The new purse is wonderful with two zippered compartments on the outside, a snapped flap also on the outside, and three deep zippered compartments that open from the top. In addition, inside two of the large compartments, there is a small zippered compartment in the lining.

I eagerly started arranging things in each compartment for ease in finding objects. Car keys in one of the outside zippered compartments, date book under the snapped flap, billfold and cosmetics in one of the bigger middle compartments, club books and checkbooks in another, and items like rain bonnets and Kleenex packets in the third.

I was very organized and efficient when I picked up my purse to go to town. I must have turned it a different direction when I picked it up because the car keys were not in the compartment where I thought I put them. After undoing several zippers, I found them on the opposite side.

A quick stop for a Dr. Pepper also found me searching frantically for the billfold, which I put thoughtfully in one of the middle sections. But I couldn't remember which section.

I left that zipper undone a little as a clue the next time I needed my billfold, but since the next thing I needed was not in that section, I began another hunt.

I thought that my telephone and address book would be safest in the inside small zippered compartment, but I discovered that there were more of those than I first noticed. It took several tries to get to the telephone number I needed. But it was safe in its little nest!

This new bag is slightly larger than the old one. When I walked down aisles in the stores, I had to be careful not to bump other shoppers with my bag. I have never been able to keep a shoulder strap on my shoulder where it belongs. I try it, and just as I lean forward to pick up something or shake hands with a friend, the bag comes toppling down onto my lower arm, making me either drop what I am picking up, or I hit my friend's hand with my heavy bag. Therefore, I selected this new bag because it has reasonably large handles to put over my arm, but not long enough for the shoulder position. That style works well most of the time unless I am carrying several packages at once, and then the size of the bag can interfere with my efficiency.

I have read that you should never carry a purse by its handles in your hand when your arm is hanging straight at your side. It is supposed to make you look dowdy as well as make you an easier prey for purse snatchers. Heeding that warning, I carry mine over a bent arm, leaving only one hand free to do other things, such as open doors or hold a child's hand. So here I go bumping into folks who come near me, struggling to find the right compartment for whatever it is that I need at the moment, and, at times, looking definitely dowdy when I change the position of my arm. But my purse is nice, shiny, and black. And it holds a lot, if I can ever find it all.

Four-Buckle Galoshes and Down-Filled Jackets

We've recently enjoyed the beauty of a deep snowfall. The trees and ground were covered with nature's frosting, and all the country looked like a Christmas card. Everywhere I looked there was another glorious sight.

That is until I looked inside the houses. Inside each home that had a child or adult who went outside there was the same scene. Boots or shoes dripping snow just inside the door, gloves or mittens laid on registers or by a stove, and coats and jackets draped over chairs to dry off decorated every living room or kitchen. The odor of wet wool dominated the whole house.

Even though this is the current situation, I thought about those years when we didn't have some of the more convenient clothing and when appliances (such as clothes dryers) were not available.

I remember the cumbersome four-buckle overshoes worn over regular shoes that usually had at least one broken clasp. My children detested them and avoided wearing them if at all possible. For less protection, we had rubbers that fit over shoes but were no higher than the actual shoes.

Trying to put them on a reluctant child was a real challenge. If the child were small enough to sit on my lap, I could pull the rubbers on over the shoes fairly easily. But an older child, especially one who didn't want to wear them, created a very different situation. The rubbers had to be put on the toe part of the shoe tightly, then eased up over the heels. Children often developed limpitis when I was pushing the rubbers onto their feet, making everyone very irritated.

Another hassle was the argument over long stockings, leggings, or snowpants. My children wore bulky snowpants, which chaffed between the thighs but were fairly easy to put on.

In my own childhood, long heavy stockings were the winter wear that I detested. They came in two colors, a flesh tone for everyday and white for dress up. These ribbed stockings were held up with garters, if you were lucky, or were fastened to a queer type of underpant. These garments had pear-shaped fasteners with a knobbed flap that held the stocking top as it was secured into the larger side of the fastener. When the stockings got wet above the galoshes or rubbers, you had damp legs for the rest of the day or until body heat dried them out.

As soon as I got away from the house, I rolled these stockings down and tried to tighten them so they wouldn't droop all over my shoes. As I got older, I was allowed to wear knee socks that had a flap at the top under which I put garters or an elastic band where it would not show. Since we always wore dresses, knee socks left a lot of bare leg under our skirts that was exposed to the elements. For Sunday best, richer children wore leggings, tight dressy leg coverings, with a matching coat. Thankfully, I escaped having to wear long underwear.

I don't remember any hooded clothing until much later. My wintertime wear usually included a neck scarf to protect the area between the coat and hat. I often lost this scarf, along with gloves or mittens, or left it at school.

Today I will go out into the snowy world in a downfilled coat with an attached hood, Isotoner gloves for easy driving, a stylish pair of plastic-lined boots, slacks, and a dressy sweatshirt. I will be well dressed, yet comfortable and warm. I will enjoy the cold and snow. But when I get back home, I will still have a pair of wet boots, a damp coat, and some wet gloves (unless I resist throwing that one snowball). I will spread these around the house to dry out before my next outing.

Some things don't change all that much.

Maybe I'm a Dirty Old Woman

After reading what I said about the baggy clothing style of young men and boys today, my son Mark accused me of being out of sync with modern trends. I may be.

But at any age we are entitled to our preferences in style; I don't happen to like the baggy pants that drag the ground and show three inches of boxer shorts at the waist. I don't have to wear them, and if those that do wear them are happy, then it is none of my concern. But I don't have to like it.

I don't like the style of the current basketball players with their baggy shorts flopping around their knees.

In the old days, I enjoyed seeing the men in their shorter shorts that fit closer to the body. It looks like they would be more comfortable; they certainly showed off the physique better.

Maybe instead of being out of sync with modern trends, I am now a dirty old woman who likes to see clothes that fit.

I feel the same way about women's and girl's clothing. I prefer a fitted dress or slacks to those that hang loose. There are some exceptions, and the comfort of the wearer is really the most important thing.

In 1946 when women's styles changed from wartime styles of fairly short skirts to the new look, I got skirts that were four inches longer. Some women or girls added ruffles or tiers to the bottom of their skirts to meet the new style. We all thought we had to wear the same length of dress. Schools even enforced rules of how long a dress should be.

That was really silly. I applaud the women today who wear their skirts any length they want. The interesting thing is they are all in style. I like some of the lengths better than others, both on myself and on other people.

One of the pluses about being my age is that I can get away with almost any style. No one notices or cares.

And, I fail to see what is so terrible about double-knit that was popular a few years back. Now it is a no-no. Many of us still wear it because it is comfortable.

The son who critiqued my column went through a period when his clothing and hair style weren't our choice. He agrees that we were tolerant of him then.

His two fine sons wear the baggy styles I was describing; I am tolerant of them and all the others. But I don't have to like it. The way I see it this is my chance to repay my kids for the times when they made remarks such as, "Mom, you're not going to wear *that* to town, are you?" I'll admit this came more often from the youngest daughter than from this son.

Though she enjoyed shopping with me because I had charge cards, sometimes she didn't want to walk beside me in the malls because my slacks were too short. Now in her maturity, she has decided that well-aired ankles are good since the extra tall sizes she needs are more expensive.

Though each of us at some time may verge on being out of sync with modern trends, mainly it is a matter of taste. We can taste all sorts of things, but we don't have to like them. We can say that we don't like them and not feel embarrassed about our preferences.

But maybe it would be better not to put it in the paper that Mark reads!

Fried Chicken or Quiche?

This week I have the responsibility of choosing the menu for a catered meal. In looking at the options I have to choose from, I couldn't help but think how our tastes in foods have changed, or enlarged, since my childhood days.

In those times, fried chicken, roast beef, baked ham, and beans and cornbread were usual meals for the family or for company. Breakfast usually was biscuits and gravy as well as eggs and bacon or sausage. A light meal could be leftover cornbread and milk. The vegetables for the main meal depended on what was fresh in the garden or was available from the cellar. One dish that was very common was stewed tomatoes, cooked with hunks of bread, and always green beans, either fresh or canned, corn, and potatoes. Though I never served potatoes for breakfast, many did.

Can you remember when you first heard of pizza? I can't be sure, but I think the first time was when I was an older teenager visiting in New York City. A man in a chef's hat was tossing pizza crust in the window of an Italian restaurant as we walked by. I was fascinated but never dreamed that in my middle age-plus years, pizza would be a staple of my diet.

Then there's quiche. I first tasted quiche about twenty years ago at a special luncheon and immediately fell in love with the taste.

Lasagna was unknown to me until my more mature years. All the goodies you can buy at a Mexican restaurant today were something I only read about.

Down the aisles of any grocery store are many selections in the pasta area and shelves devoted to foods that I had never experienced until the last quarter century.

This abundance of food choices brings up concerns. Every day we read about a food that isn't good for us, is contaminated, or has caused a problem because of improper cooking.

Back in the days when we had our main meal at noon and left much of the food on the table covered by a cloth until supper, I don't remember hearing about food poisoning, but perhaps we didn't know what it was.

In those days, we enjoyed high-fat food, ate heartily, and even corrected the children if they left the fatty pieces on their plates.

We ate lots of eggs because they were cheap, and many people had their own hens.

We drank quantities of whole milk and put lots of homemade butter on our vegetables and bread.

A diet like this would put dietitians in shock today, but in our more active lifestyles, we survived, even thrived, on these foods.

Thinking of all these varieties of things to eat

brings me back to my task of choosing a menu for our meeting. Lasagna, Quiche, and Chicken Divan were all possibilities. I hate to show my ignorance by asking what Chicken Divan is. I thought a divan was something you sat on. Maybe then this is pressed chicken?

I wonder what would happen if I asked for a meal of fried chicken, fried potatoes, stewed tomatoes with bread, slaw, cornbread, and apple pie? Sounds good, doesn't it? But I'll probably go with the lasagna. Even in middle age-plus years, we need to keep up with the times.

A Really Cool Story

Our ice maker is giving us trouble again. We fuss and fume about all the bother when the ice won't pop out into our glasses as we push the lever on the outside of the refrigerator door. Sometimes we have to open the door and go to all the trouble of getting the ice out of the container or repositioning the lever.

Such problems didn't exist for us in earlier years. If we were lucky enough to have an icebox, our problems were much messier.

The icebox of my childhood was filled every two days by Riley Kafer. He drove a big truck loaded with blocks of ice packed in straw and covered with a tarp to keep the sun from melting his wares before he reached the homes on his route. We put a card in the window which told him how much ice we wanted that day. We always turned up the side that said a hundred because, in our big family, we served many iced drinks and opened the icebox door often enough to melt ice quickly.

I remember the way he carried in the ice with tongs while resting the big cake of ice on his upper leg as he walked. He wore a divided apron that was rubberized to keep him from becoming completely wet before the end of his route.

The ice he delivered was from the ice house in town. I also remember some homemade ice that he cut from his lake in the winter and stored in a barn with hay and sawdust for insulation. Though not fit for putting in drinks, we used it in ice boxes and for freezing ice cream. I'm not sure we kids were supposed to go inside the barn filled with ice, but we did. It was a wonderful place for a summertime playhouse.

Sometimes, if we had company or were planning to make ice cream in between his visits, we made a special trip to town to the commercial ice house ourselves.

It was fun watching the ice slide out of the little L-shaped building through a little door that had rubber flaps hanging over the opening. It slid down onto the wooden platform where a stout boy hoisted it on the bumper of our car for the ride home.

By the time we reached home, the ice had melted into the frame of the bumper enough that its shape was impressed into the ice.

The biggest problem with this type of icebox was what happened as the ice melted. We set a big green dishpan under a wooden flap at the bottom of the icebox.

I said it was big, but somehow it was never big enough or perhaps our memory was too short, for we had to hold many impromptu mopping sessions because someone didn't empty the pan before going to bed. Even if we did remember, carrying it from the icebox through the door to the yard without spilling part or all of the cold water on us or the floor was a challenge. We always poured this nice soft water on my mother's petunia bed, which, thankfully, was fairly near the back door.

To get to our homes, ice took a lot of work. It was moved from the lake to the barn or from the ice plant to the truck. It was covered with straw, sawdust, and tarpaulin, and then rested on knees, or slid across wooden platforms before riding on the bumper of a car down a dirt road. Whichever route, it was deposited in a well-used icebox. None of this hampered our enjoyment of chopping off a small hunk to suck on or to put in lemonade.

I guess it didn't hurt us because here we are, several decades later, still hale and hearty and able to fuss about this modern convenience we have that doesn't always work just right.

Pasterurized, Homogenized, Bottled, and Cooled

I recently stopped at the dairy case at Woods Supermarket to select products to buy. I could choose between whole milk, 2% milk, 1% milk, 1/2% milk, skim milk, buttermilk, half and half, whipping cream, sour cream, cottage cheese, sour cream with onions, chocolate milk, dips, and specialized milk for those with digestive problems.

I have always liked milk. When I was a child, there was a pitcher of milk regularly on the table in addition to our own glassful. But it has not always been as easy to provide milk.

During our summers on the farm, we bought a gallon of milk each day from Mrs. John Welty. Her milk was rich, raw, Jersey milk with lots of cream. We had a little blue, enamel gallon bucket that we carried to the Welty house each morning. Mrs. Welty dipped the milk from a crock into the bucket for us to take home and put in the ice box.

If we were lucky, we could drive the mile to our neighbor. But I have also walked, have ridden a bicycle with the filled bucket swinging precariously from the handlebars, and have even ridden Princess Peggy, our saddle horse.

In the winters when we lived in Washington, D.C., we had four quarts of milk delivered on our front porch each morning. We carried this milk inside. It was pasteurized but not homogenized, and we removed about two inches of cream off the top to put into our cream pitchers before we poured the milk for drinking. In cold weather, we often stepped outside the door to see about one inch of frozen cream sticking up above the bottle with the cardboard milk bottle cap perching on top. I wonder now how many cats got a little breakfast from this exposed treat, but we didn't worry about it at the time. We cut off the protruding frozen cream to place in the cream pitcher and let the rest thaw in the bottle. After emptying a bottle, we washed it out, put in a note for the milkman, if there was any change in our usual order, and put it back out on the porch for the dairy to use again.

After my husband and I married, we lived on a farm in Cedar County, Missouri, with our own milk cow. Though Lester did the milking, I had the fun of keeping the milk utensils clean and sanitary. Since we then had children, we wanted to pasteurize the milk, even though we had our own healthy cow. We used a little aluminum pasteurizer that held a gallon bucket. This method was automatic and except for the numerous spills that occurred when I put the bucket in or took it out, I had little trouble.

During the pasteurizing process, the cream

rose to the top; we skimmed off a nice leathery inch or so of cream from each gallon. That's where the fun began—trying to convert that cream into butter using my electric mixer. Because of my efforts, our children thought our kitchen was supposed to have cream polka-dotted wallpaper.

When we moved to Vernon County, there was a period when my nine-year-old son and I had to do the milking when my Lester was gone for the summer college term. Poor old Sugar, our Jersey, went dry a little early that year. I'm sure it was to avoid our attempts at milking. Our son did much better than I, but then I didn't really want to learn too well. If I knew how, I'd have no excuse for avoiding that chore!

When I buy my milk tonight at the store, I will not mourn the past but will enjoy making a leisurely selection from the many products that are now available, already pasteurized, homogenized, bottled, and cooled.

Lemonade

Lemonade sure tastes good on these hot summer days. Each week I usually fix it for several meals or for in-between drinks. Each time I make a pitcherful, I remember how we made it when I was a child. In our family, it was my job on most days to make the drink because the older ones were working on bigger projects.

I started by rolling four or five lemons on the kitchen cabinet to make the lemons juicier. I did this with my hands for about a minute with each lemon. Then I cut them in half. Using a twisting wrist motion on a glass squeezer, I got out every bit of juice. Since we did not use the pulp, I carefully held back the seeds and pulp as I poured the juice into a large pitcher.

After squeezing all the lemons, I did the same for two or three oranges and poured the juice in the pitcher. I added sugar and filled the pitcher with water. We stirred the water, juice, and sugar together until there was no more tell-tale sugar in the bottom.

At the last minute, I added the ice, after chipping some off the big hunk in the icebox. I didn't want to use too much or there wouldn't

be enough ice to keep our food cold until Mr.
Kafer brought another hundred pounds the next
day. After I chipped off the ice, we washed it
before putting it into glasses and pitchers. That
caused a little more melting of the precious cooler.

Finished with this, I loaded a tray with glasses
of ice and the pitcher of lemonade and tried to
get through the back door without spilling any
of it. I proudly took it to the family members who
were resting after work in the shade of the elm
trees.

It tasted very good, and I didn't mind making
the drink because Ellen and I had our own treat
we made with the lemon rind after squeezing
out the juice. We filled the rinds with sugar,
poured in a little water, and then sucked the
lemon-flavored sugar water from the rinds until
there was very little left of the peeling. I haven't
tried that treat in my adult years, but I still
remember the wonderful flavor we enjoyed with
all that sugar!

Lemonade today is simple. I fill a pitcher with
water, pour in a capful of lemonade mix, take
cubes of ice from the refrigerator, and enjoy my
drink. I have no fruit peelings to carry off, no
sugar spilled on the cabinet, and no ice dripping
across the kitchen floor.

But I did have some sweet memories of a cool
drink shared with my family on a hot summer
day.

3

Mr. Edison Would Be Amazed!

Things do not change; we change

Henry David Thoreau 1850

Our Love Affair with the Automobile

Our nation has had a love affair with automobiles since the turn of the century. My generation has experienced this love through many changes in our cars. Many of the changes are very welcome. But I miss the running boards.

Early automobiles had running boards on each side to step up on before entering the car. These running boards were also used for carrying bulky or dirty objects without putting them inside. Most cars did not have trunks then; the few that did had a box-like appendage on the back that was not formed as part of the car's body. Therefore, we put articles on the running board and tied them to the running lights that protruded in front of the front seat windows.

One of the best things about running boards was that extra passengers could stand on them. With the windows rolled, the boys could insert their arms around the bar between the front and back seats and could hold on securely and ride along with the inside passengers. I remember many times when a couple of extra people stood on the running board on each side of the car as we drove to a neighborhood function. Of course, we didn't do this at high speeds or on well-traveled roads. However, I do remember one instance when I was visiting the home of my future husband in Taney County, Missouri, (long before the tourist boom made the area easily accessible). After meeting my bus, Lester stood on the running board of his brother's coupe while we drove the twenty miles over graveled, dusty roads from Forsyth to Protem because we had more people than the seat of the coupe would hold. As I remember it, he was also holding a flashlight because the headlights of this wartime car weren't working.

Some of my earliest memories of cars include watching my brother crank the engine to get it started. Someone had to sit in the driver's seat and move the spark lever to the right position at the right time. Occasionally, I was the only one available for this job, and I never seemed to get the timing of this procedure in sync with my brother's efforts.

Shifting of the early cars had a different sequence from the four-or-five-on-the-floor cars of today. We started in first gear at the upper left of the gear shifts.

Then we proceeded to second, which was lower left, and finally into high gear, which was upper right of the gear shift. Reverse gear was on the lower right side.

I also remember accelerators that were not rectangular pedals but were small, metal, round pedals about the size of a silver dollar.

When I drove as a very young driver (eleven), I had trouble reaching this pedal and keeping my foot on the slippery accelerator.

Another difference in the cars was the space between the front and back seats. Our family of ten all rode in the car together, even on the three- or four-day trips from Nevada to Washington, D.C. Three or four would sit in front, four would sit on the back seat, and the two others would sit on folding camp stools in between the front and back seats. I was usually the fourth one—on someone's lap—in one of the seats. In today's cars, I am lucky to find room for my knees between the front and back seats, much less have room for a stool with a child on it.

I am happy in my little Mercury Tracer with reclining bucket seats, cruise control, air-conditioning and heater, and a big streamlined trunk.

But I would still like to have a running board.

Hang Up and Try Again

Last night I counted the telephones in our house. There's no spot in our small house that is more than a step or two away from a phone. When we bought our modular home, it didn't have towel rods or toilet paper holders, but it had a phone in each room. When we brought phones from our previous home, we had lots of opportunities for conversations, courtesy of Ma Bell.

In my recent travels, I've noticed passing motorists with a phone in hand, talking as they drive down the interstate. I see businessmen in restaurants using a phone while eating. Truck stops always have the opportunity for phone calls at the tables, on the counter, and along the walls.

All these phones make me wonder if this is a convenience or a burden. We did seem to have relatively happy lives before we had the convenience of instant phone connections.

I remember the big old wooden phone we had hanging on our wall in the kitchen when I was a child. We were on a party line with Mrs. Horn, the Watsons, Eaton, Maples, Halcombs, and Weltys. Each had a personal ring--ours two shorts and a long.

I was disappointed when hearing two shorts, signaling the Eatons. We always knew some neighbors listened in. At times that was convenient.

When a child forgot a message or mixed it up, we called Mrs. Horn to get the correct information.

To reach Central, we rang one long, and the operator connected us to other lines and other towns. A real human being (usually someone we knew) staffed the Central switchboard and provided helpful tidbits such as, "Mrs. Jones isn't home today but is at the Browns' if you need her."

The little crank on the side of the phone case wasn't as convenient as the touchtone phones of today, but when trying to call home recently using my phone credit card, I had to punch six numbers to get the company that issued my card, another eleven numbers to indicate whom I was calling, and then ten more for my credit card number, and finally the last four secret PIN numbers. I found myself longing for the nice lady at Central who could help me out. This was especially true when after all that number punching, I got a shrill recorded message, "If you would like to place a call, please hang up and try again!"

I guess we middle age-plus folk don't appreciate each modern advance like we should, but much can be said for the friendliness of the old ways, too. I could go on more with this idea, but I must stop to make a phone call.

The Fun of Flat Tires

How long has it been since you changed a flat tire? I mean really changed it yourself? When I notice a low tire, I use the compressed air cylinder to air it up and then drive to my favorite station where the attendant puts the car up on the lift and puts sudsy water on the tire until he finds the leak and seals it in a second with some kind of plug. Even the bill isn't too bad.

Those in my generation had experiences with flat tires that weren't so pleasant. During World War II, tires were so hard to get that we weren't allowed to have a spare tire. My sister Ellen and I were taking our sister Miriam to the train station in McBaine, Missouri, from Columbia where she was visiting us while we were in a summer term at Missouri University. To get on the *Katy* train very late at night, we had to drive fifteen miles from Columbia to this tiny town to catch her train.

We made the trip, put Miriam on the train, and started back. Suddenly, we heard the ominous sound of air hissing. Sure enough, the right rear tire was flat. We had all the provisions and the instructions, but we had never attempted to mend a punctured inner tube, replace it in the tire casing, inflate it, and remount it. Since we had no other choice, we began. Jacking up the car and removing the wheel was easy since we'd done that many times, but getting the inner tube out of the casing was tricky. We must have punctured the inner tube a second time during the process because after we got it out, used the little rasping tool in the kit to roughen up the area of the hole we found, and glued on a patch, the inner tube still wouldn't hold air. We repeated the patching process to no avail. Then we found the second hole and went through the patching process again.

During this time, several cars passed, but no one stopped to assist because we hid in the ditch as they passed, thinking it was not safe for two girls to accept help at that time of night (or morning by now). When we saw headlights, we pushed all tell-tale signs of what we were doing out of sight and then got down in the deep ditch to hide.

Thinking back, there was probably more danger from snakes or something in the ditch than from any hard-working person who was driving to town very early in the morning.

After applying the third patch, reinserting the inner tube, and inflating it with a hand pump, we put the wheel back on the car and reached Columbia just in time to clean up and go to our first hour classes. Some good old days weren't so sweet.

Or Maybe We Could Buy a Rooster

I sometimes get upset with myself for my reliance on television, even for telling time. I know that it is six-thirty when *Wheel of Fortune* comes on. If the news is delayed by a late-running sports event, I get upset if the weather doesn't come on at ten-fifteen so I can go on to bed.

As a child, I listened for the *Katy Flyer* to pass on the nearby railroad tracks to alert my parents that it was bedtime. Our one clock in the house struck the hours so if the train was late, the old Seth Thomas would begin the bedtime ritual when my parents heard the clock striking nine.

When in college, I listened for the chimes on Memorial Tower at Missouri University to keep me timely, especially to avoid any problem with getting in after hours at my boarding house.

It seems that all my early life I usually had one ear open for some sound to signify the time.

When we married and had children, we had the responsibility of trying to get our babies to get hungry by the clock.

Then parents were trained to believe we would

ruin a child for life if we gave in and fed the child a few minutes before the prescribed feeding time. During those years, I kept one eye on the clock and the other on the ready-to-warm bottle. Thankfully, by the time our youngest child arrived, the rules had relaxed somewhat.

Later, when I worked outside the home, my time was regulated by working hours and by the growing children's school activities. I needed no outside clues, for time stared me in the face at any given moment, especially since we also had a full church life with my husband being a minister.

Now in semi-retirement years, I am back to a more relaxed mode. Even though we have clocks in every room of the house, I seldom consult them and depend on such things as the television.

Lester consults the sun for the time, but that changes too quickly for me, since I can't believe how dark the mornings are in the fall when it should be only midsummer at most. Then we always had different ways of remembering time. I remember which child was a baby when a certain incident happened. Lester remembers which car we owned at the time. As we progress into middle age-plus, I hope I'll be able to hear my time signals. If not, I may have to go back to methods learned in parenting--eat when we're hungry and sleep when we're sleepy and not worry about whether it fits in with the schedule of the rest of the world.

Or maybe we could just buy a rooster.

Goodbye Dial, Hello Punch One

I need to change the way I use the telephone. The new programs that people can have on their telephones have me all fouled up, so I will learn new methods in my calling.

I didn't realize that when people had caller ID on *their* phone that they could tell how many times I had called them. Some Sunday afternoons when I am making long distance calls to my children and they are not at home, I try again in an hour or so. After a while, if I don't get them, I begin to wonder what they could be doing to be gone so long. I keep trying to call. My idea is that if they are not home, it won't cost me anything to keep trying, and if they have returned, then I can talk to them and no one will need to know that I spent the afternoon trying to reach them.

Now when Michael does come home and looks at the caller ID to find that I have called ten times that afternoon, he thinks there must be a real emergency. He doesn't realize that Mom was just being a little too nosy for her own good! The problem is I don't know who does have caller ID. Because of that, I need to change another practice. When I am working on a project and need to know a detail, I often call a friend who might have a quick answer. But if my friend isn't home, I call another person who might possibly give me the information. Often I will call four or five persons before getting results. That is fine, I think. I haven't bothered anyone except the one who answered, but in a few hours my husband gets a confusing phone call from someone saying they are answering his call. He has no idea what is going on until the caller says our number (which is listed in my husband's name) appeared on their caller ID. By then I had almost forgotten what I called about. I have bothered several people whom I called not knowing they had this contraption on their phone. In addition, I put Lester out on a limb since the ID identifies him and not me.

We have an answering machine which has been very helpful at times, but when we recently went on a trip and left the machine on, we returned to find the thing blinking its heart out with messages. On some machines, you can call while away to retrieve messages. Our machine does not work that way, or if it does, we don't know how it works. With an answering machine, friends called while we were away and left messages, thinking that we would receive them. Once we were gone two weeks and most of the messages needed answering well before we returned.

In a way, I'm glad we don't have the capability

of calling in to retrieve messages. We would have to make a bunch of long distance calls on our vacation and conduct business we would rather forget for a while. However, next time we are both out of town, I will turn off our answering machine.

We have several phones, but some of them are not touchtone phones. Invariably, when I make a call that needs a touchtone, I have picked up the wrong phone. It is maddening to sit and listen to all the, "If you want to reach...punch 1, if you want to...punch 2." As a last resort, I get a real live human to talk to, but by then I have probably forgotten what I called about.

Now I am wondering if I call someone with caller ID and the line is busy, if I keep punching the redial button until I reach them, do they have a record of that? I use the redial very often when I call a list of names, so that I don't have to clutter up my mind with a bunch of phone numbers, but sometimes when I do finally reach the person, I have forgotten whom I called. It is embarrassing. I have had people reply, "Who are you calling?" Then I have to fes up that I really don't know.

Progress is wonderful, but some of us need retraining for this new age. I don't expect an operator at Central any longer, but it would be nice to talk to some real people somewhere along the line. I am still not used to having other people's telephone machines checking up on my dialing habits. If you agree with me, please call and punch #. Maybe it will pound out some of our frustrations!

Making Hay in the Sunshine

Sunday night I returned from being gone for several days and was rejoicing that some of my responsibilities were over or winding down. I was thinking about how much I will enjoy the summer free time and relaxation. Then I opened the mail.

Staring at me from the top of the pile was a special J. C. Penney's Back-to-School catalog, and it isn't even the middle of July, and we're asked to buy for back to school. Even though my children are grown, just the thought of our grandchildren and their parents having to start planning for school already lessened my feelings of freedom.

For me, summer signifies a time to be free from schedules, to spend time on productive activities, such as sitting outside and watching the clouds or reading a good book while lying in the shade.

Many educators are advocating year round school terms and shorter periodic vacations. Working parents and single parents like this arrangement. In some neighborhoods, this system provides parents with child care for longer periods of the year. I understand this need, but part of me yearns for each child to have the opportunity to spend a carefree summer with time to dream, to experiment with ideas, and to enjoy the outdoors.

Rural children are always kept busy in the summer helping with farm duties. Sturdy boys could always earn extra money bucking hay bales for neighbors. Now with the huge hay bales that can be moved only by a truck or tractor, these jobs are scarce. Going further back in time, instead of helping get hay bales in a barn, boys would have used a pitchfork to fork loose hay up onto a hay wagon to take to the barn and pitch up into the hayloft or form it into a haystack in the pasture. If there was a big amount of hay, a hayfork from a pulley at the top of the barn took the hay from wagons into the loft. A horse supplied the power as it walked forward and back, raising fork loads of hay to loft level where it was propelled inside by a continuing rail until it reached the place to drop the load. This operation required several people, both in the hay fields and in the barnyard.

Now the hay bale can stay in the field until needed or be moved by one person on a tractor or truck where livestock eat it right off the bale.

Since we all need more money to buy those bargains in the Back to School catalog, it seems that my wishes for summer activities will only be memories of those of us who are middle age-plus.

Curled Up with a Computer

I hope the computer age doesn't eliminate books completely. I can't imagine that reading the text of a book from a screen while seated in front of a computer could ever have the satisfying effects of curling up with a good book in an easy chair.

Those who read for a while in bed certainly don't want to have a laptop computer in bed with them nor would those who read while traveling on a train or plane. In fact, there are some fears that electronic devices might interfere with the operation of a plane.

My love for books started very early. Two of our aunts often gave Ellen and me books as gifts. We each treasured a large (probably 11" by 13") book with colored illustrations called *The Real Story Book*. I think Ellen still has it. One of the stories told about a family of quail that was trying to teach the young to fly before the farmer cut the wheat field, thus destroying their cover. Whenever I heard the familiar bobwhite call, I imagined it was that family of quail working with their little ones.

I always asked my mother to read another

story about the crooked man with the crooked hat. Her tongue got twisted over the words, and I would laugh delightedly.

An early book that is impressed in my mind is the *Baby Ray Primer* that my mother used to teach me to read. Even when I attended kindergarten, she still liked to teach me at home after the morning class was over. Since time alone with her was rare in such a large family, I loved these sessions. I still get a thrill from remembering her praise when I memorized a poem in the book. (I still know it, too!)

I suppose a child in the lap of someone at a computer could bring the same results, but I can remember fondly clutching the book to my body as I ran to play after one of our reading sessions. A computer doesn't cuddle easily.

Each summer at the farm, I always reread my favorite books. We had different books at home in Washington, D.C., but since I was in school and had other activities, I didn't read as much from the family library in the winter. Instead, I used the public library weekly.

The Tenleytown Branch of the D.C. library had a wonderful section for young readers. I checked out the limit of three books almost every week. Part of this ritual included a tearful plea to an older brother to take me back to the library at night because the books were due.

Even though the library was across Wisconsin Avenue from Janney Elementary School where I attended, it never occurred to me to take the books to school and return them on the way home. It was more fun to manipulate Harold into taking me back in the evening. Part of the fun was having time alone with this big brother.

The books I loved to read each summer included *The Lost Prince*, *Rebecca of Sunnybrook Farm*, *Amarylis of Clothesline Alley*, *Girl of the Limberlost*, and later the Willa Cather books. Many of these books are still at our family home, but others have been added to the bookshelves of each of our family members.

My father always wrote his name in his large, bold style in the front of each of his books. Sometimes he added the date or who presented the book to him. This makes the volume even more of a treasure.

One benefit of the computer is that much reading can be stored in one little machine, whereas the bookcases and shelves in our homes take up valuable space. But I like the looks of a wall covered with shelves of books. I notice that interviews on TV are often conducted in front of a bookcase full of books. I am not the only one who enjoys that appearance of learning.

Now that my writing can be read on a web page (vcrecord.com), I should appreciate computers even more. But after reading it on the computer, you can't recycle it to line the bottom of your bird cage. I guess you could hit the delete button if you wanted to.

Time on Your Hands and Everywhere Else

The new Chamber of Commerce brochure about Nevada features a good picture of the courthouse tower and clock. This brings back many memories because that clock was an important landmark in my youth.

Clocks were not as prevalent then as they are now, and children rarely had watches. Some boys had pocket watches to wear in their overalls, if they had the ninety-eight cents to buy them. My sisters and I never had our own wrist watches until we graduated from high school. That was the traditional present in our family. It was a very good Elgin watch (which I still have, but do not wear).

It was important to budget our time in town by looking at the courthouse clock or listening for it to strike the hour or half hour. Since we could see it from almost any store in town, we depended on this clock to keep us on time.

I also used the clock for another personal purpose. When I arrived at our farm home late after a date, often the next morning, my mother asked what time it was when I got in. I could truthfully answer her that it was ten o'clock when we passed the courthouse clock and that I couldn't see the time on the clock on the mantle in our living room because I didn't have a light. I neglected to say what else we might have done after we passed the courthouse clock, but the two statements were true.

At that time, we had only the one clock in our home. The Seth Thomas striking clock still sits on the clock mantle where my father put it over ninety years ago. Now numerous electric and battery clocks supplement this family treasure.

I recently counted the clocks in my own home. We have two in our bedroom, one for each side of the bed to use as individual alarms. In addition, we each have a wind-up travel alarm nearby. There is also a clock in each of the two bathrooms, one on the oven, the microwave, and the VCR, which flashes 12:00 more than any other time. We have a large battery-powered clock on the living room wall in addition to a pendulum clock, a new bird song battery clock, and an ornamental wall clock. In the guest room, there are two clocks for the convenience of visitors and for me to use at the computer. Naturally, Lester needs more than one upstairs in his study, and each of our vehicles has a clock on the dashboard.

My family home has the added security of a sundial on the lawn. During daylight savings time it is one hour off, but it still gives us time information. Just in case we are away from all of these, we each wear a watch. When I get up in the morning, I reach for my glasses and my watch.

So with all these time pieces, are we ever late for a meeting? Of course we are. The difference is we are very much aware of each minute we are late by glancing at all the clocks and watches around us as we rush to our appointments.

I wonder if middle age-plus years will eventually give me time to forget about time? Probably I will always glance at the courthouse clock whenever I pass it, even if I'm not in a hurry. I never know when I might need a good excuse!

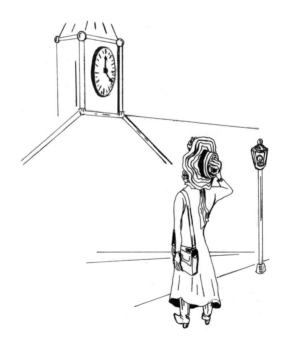

On the Cutting Edge

I cut my toenails this morning. Normally that would not be an item to write about, but while I was cutting my toenails, I began thinking about how they were cut when I was a child.

We had one pair of scissors in the house. To me, they seemed to have very long blades. My mother used those big scissors to cut my fingernails and toenails.

Later, I remember, she had some little curved scissors for fingernails, but they weren't used for toenails. I was out on my own before I saw or used fingernail or toenail clippers.

I did a serious scientific survey on other middle age-plus people to see when they first knew about or used clippers for nail care. (Well, I asked three other people.) I learned that soldiers in World War II could buy clippers in the PX. That was the first time that my respondents used this modern convenience.

Returning home, they then introduced the item to their families back home when on leave or after the war.

Since my survey is not all inclusive, perhaps there are some of you who have had different experiences.

I asked Lester how he trimmed his nails when he was a child. He said he used a knife. Other men reported using a knife, too. I have no idea if my brothers used knives or if they also used Mama's big scissors.

Today we have scissors in a drawer in the kitchen. I also have one pair I use for quick sewing jobs, another pair in my desk drawer, and Lester has at least two in his loft office.

As a joke one Christmas, we got him a huge pair of scissors with a chain attached because he always complained that one of us carried off his scissors.

I also have a small collapsible pair that I carry in my purse, one in my cosmetic case for travel, and I think there are some old ones out where tools are supposed to be kept.

In addition to all this cutting apparatus, I have both fingernail and toenail clippers, the curved manicure scissors, and an old key ring that has some dull clippers on the chain for decoration.

Each of my children had their own clippers when they were home, and I suppose they have some in their own homes now.

All these scissors are a far cry from the one big pair my mother had when she was raising the eight of us.

When we started school, one of the items we put in our book bag was a pair of round-ended scissors. I remember the joy of having this small pair of blunt scissors all my own. I used these scissors to cut out my many paper dolls and to make snow flakes from folded notebook paper, and I more than likely had some unauthorized uses, too.

When I took clothing construction in college, the professor said there should be a separate pair of scissors for sewing that was not used for anything else. That was when I turned into a multiple scissors owner.

Now one thing keeps bothering me. Why are scissors plural? We even call them a pair of scissors. If we are talking about a pair of mules (for instance), that makes sense. There are two animals in the pair. But a pair of scissors is only one instrument with two blades. Is each blade then a scissor? The only entry in my dictionary that has the word without the -s ending is a verb meaning to cut. It is confusing.

I don't have much time to worry about it. I need to run some errands. I will put on a blouse and a pair of pants and hurry to town.

4

Philosophies from Where I Stand

The farther backward you can look, the farther forward you are likely to see.

Winston Churchill

Becoming a Ridiculously Young Great-Grandmother

I am sitting in my favorite rocker with a beautiful baby girl in my arms while she is noisily drinking from a bottle. It feels natural and good. Then I remember. This baby is not my grandchild. This baby is my great-grandchild! How on earth could that be?

It was just a few years ago that I held her grandmother in my arms the same way. And only a few months ago that I cradled her mother. Time couldn't have passed that quickly. Because, you see, I am still the same age—well, more or less the same age anyway.

So how did these babies grow up so quickly? But here I am with this new one in my arms. I ponder just what relationship we will have, this little one and I. Will she think of me as a doddering old woman, or will she be smart enough to see all the benefits that this exceptionally young great-grandmother can give her?

I can tell her about so many things that no one else would know or bother to tell her. I can tell her what it was like to travel in a car with seven siblings and one or two parents in the days before air conditioning.

I can explain that there were no trunks on the cars, so all the luggage had to be put on running boards with a little collapsible gate holding everything in. (But of course, first I would have to tell her what a running board is!)

If that isn't interesting enough, I can tell her what it was like to be a teenager in wartime Washington, D.C., where we lived in a perpetual brownout and could not use the car for recreational purposes.

Do you suppose she would in interested to know that I went to my prom on a streetcar and had to go to an air-raid shelter on the way to the prom because of an air-raid drill?

Or would she like to hear some of the great songs that I grew up with? I could sing to her about Aunt Rhody whose old gray goose is dead. (I think she died in the mill pond a-standing on her head!) She would like that, wouldn't she?

Or maybe "Chickery Chick, Cha La, Cha La." Now that is a song with real meaning and lots of words. Not just repetition of the same phrase over and over like the modern songs.

I can explain the mechanics of defrosting a refrigerator, winding a clock, using a wringer washing machine, or opening and closing windows for temperature control. That should fascinate her!

Yes, this little girl will have such an advantage over other children who don't have the privilege of having such a young great-grandmother. I look down at this lucky child to see a crooked smile around the bottle nipple and realize she has finished her bottle and is wondering what this person feeding her is going to do next. Good question.

What naturally comes next is a burp. That can be managed, and since I have to wait a few years to impart this other knowledge I have been dreaming about, I will just be content now with loving her and letting her know that I can be counted on.

Whoops, what do I smell? Oh, oh! Now is the time for an incredibly young great-grandmother to get busy. I hold her carefully in my arms to rise from the rocking chair.

A little rock forward will give me a boost and make rising more graceful with this little bundle in my arms. Okay, another bigger rock forward ought to do it. Well, maybe a third!

I think maybe it would be just as well to sit here and rock a few minutes in spite of the diaper problem. Her mother is due back soon and these young great-grandmothers don't have to tell the whole world all of their problems.

Maybe we will sing a little—Three little fishes and the momma fishie too——

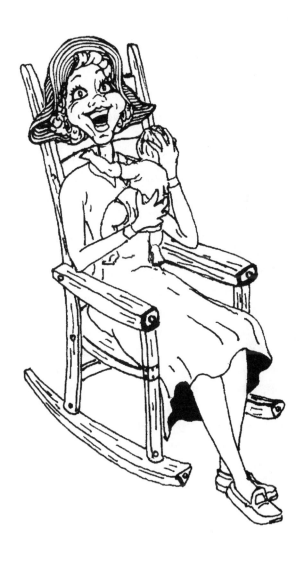

Dream Control

Now that schools are about to start again, it's about time for me to have my recurring dream. In my dream, I am walking up the hill to Woodrow Wilson High School in Washington, D.C. I hear the bell ringing and the intercom is playing a Sousa march to hurry the students inside. Knowing I'm late, I panic because I've never been late to school. And this is the first day. My schedule for my new classes is in my locker, and as I run into the big building and up the two flights of stairs to the third floor to my locker, I forget the combination. So I am late for my first class; and I don't know what my first class is. I then usually wake up, but sometimes I try unsuccessfully to find the principal's office to get some information. This vivid dream makes me dislike going into a school building that is unfamiliar to me because it brings back those feelings from the dream.

I realized lately, as I was preparing to teach a course on Our Violent Society, that I feel safest when I'm in control.

I like to drive rather than fly because even though much can happen while driving that is beyond my control, I usually can set my schedule. I can start and stop when I want to, and I can choose my companions.

My school dream bothers me because I am not in control of the situation and am helpless to get back in control.

Getting older can be like that dream. Things happen that are beyond my control. I can't do all that I used to, and I can't always remember the combination—such as where I left my watch, or what time the lady on the phone said the meeting would be. I choose my traveling companions, but they can't always go the whole way with me. So I am somewhat out of control.

But look at the things I can control. I can go to bed when I want, get up when I want, except that I keep waking up before I want to. I can watch whatever television show I want to without worrying whether it's okay for the rest of the family to see. I can dress comfortably because it's too late to make much impression on anyone anyway. And I have no need to find the principal's office.

A variation of my dream also visits me some nights. In this dream, I am going into class for the final exam, but I have not even opened the book all semester. I haven't a clue about the subject.

As I continue into the class of middle age-plus, I struggle to be in control before I have to take the test.

Old Enough to Qualify

I was traveling last weekend on a chartered bus. At one of the rest stops at a fast food restaurant, I ordered a medium soft drink. The waiter charged me only twenty-six cents. I thought he had made a mistake and asked him if that wasn't too low. He assured me that was the correct price. Thinking the owners were in the midst of some special promotion, I asked what they were celebrating. The poor young man became embarrassed and said this was the usual price. Since this wasn't what was posted on the menu above his head, I persisted with questions as he became more flustered.

It finally dawned on me. This was the price for Senior Citizens and not for everyone. I made the waiter even more ill at ease when I turned to some of my friends and announced that they could also get a drink for this price.

Since some of our bus load were young women and others not yet middle age-plus, he thought he was being put in the position of asking ages before charging for the drinks. None of us put him on that spot, so we went our way sipping on our twenty-six cent sodas.

I have often used the senior discount when it was marked on the menu, but this was the first time it had been offered to me without my asking for it. I appreciated the young man giving me this opportunity to save a few cents but was amused that he was embarrassed that he could tell that I was old enough to qualify.

Since age is something we have no control over, why should it be a source of embarrassment to be recognized as being in the older category? We do not hesitate to ask the age of a youngster. Most will proudly hold up their fingers to show us exactly how old they have become. Just when does it cease being a source of pride? And when does it become something to be ashamed of?

Each year added to our lives has brought us new experiences, knowledge, and relationships. Of course, many years also take their toll physically and mentally, but those toddlers proudly holding up three fingers also have some physical and mental limitations. Each age has its pluses and minuses, but none of us should be ashamed of our age nor should well meaning young men be ill at ease for recognizing us for the age we are.

I could write about why should I get a discount just because I am middle age-plus. Actually, my adult grandchildren need this discount more than I do.

However, I still enjoyed my twenty-six cent drink.

Even If I Ought To

I ought to have gone to a meeting today, but I stayed home. I enjoyed the day very much, but I did keep feeling that I ought to have gone to the meeting. You see, I didn't have any real responsibilities. Though it was more of a party than a meeting, I was sort of expected to be there. But I decided that in my new state of retirement I am going to retire the word "ought." I will not use it to make me feel guilty about what I could be doing with my time. I figure that by the time I am this age, I should be doing things because I want to—not because I ought to.

Some days I'd have enjoyed attending the meeting I skipped today. But today I didn't want to go. So I didn't. I realize that is making me become the type of person that I resented when I was working and probably setting up such meetings. It looks different from this side of retirement. I want to be useful. I want to help in many causes both locally and worldwide. I want to take good care of my family, my pets, myself. But I *want* to do these things. I'm not doing them because I "ought" to. I looked up the word "ought" in my crossword puzzle dictionary that I keep handy to help with the puzzles in the paper. The alternatives to "ought" include "naught" and "nought." I'm not sure what the difference between those two is, and I suppose I "ought" to go look them up in a real dictionary. But it's under three other books and a globe, and I don't want to attempt messing up things right now. Anyway, I know that the words mean nothing. So if ought is the same as nothing, then there is no reason to be concerned about something I "ought" to do. It is nothing!

Think about the word for awhile. Even the sound is annoying. Ought. It sounds like something has been left off of the word, probably because it is usually accompanied by the word you. "You ought." That sounds even uglier. It brings back memories of a teacher peering down at me or a parent calling up the stairs, "You ought to do better." "You ought to clean your room." "You ought to be like your sister." "You ought to...."

I can't remember many times when the words have had a favorable meaning. "You ought to go lie down" might be an example. After I passed the age of obligatory naps, I don't remember hearing that phrase too often when it was addressed to me. "You ought to win the contest, the game, or the prize" indicates that I probably won't even if I ought to.

"You ought to see this movie or read this book" could be another favorable example. But it does indicate that I probably missed out or wasn't quick enough to realize this myself.

It seems like I ought to be able to think of

other examples, but somehow I can't seem to.

So in my middle age-plus years, I have chosen to not respond to oughts. I will answer to "Would you like to?" or "Is it possible for you to...." but I will not answer to "You ought to." After I spent the afternoon writing, listening to classical music on PBS radio, making a few phone calls, and looking out at the beautiful day, I began wondering a little about the meeting. How had it gone? Did anyone notice that I wasn't there? Did I let my friend down by not going? Were the refreshments good?

I probably ought to call and see how things went. Maybe I ought to apologize to my friend for skipping out on her. Or perhaps I ought to pretend that I forgot the meeting and apologize for missing it.

Whatever I do, I ought to do it quickly, so I won't feel guilty all night. I think I know what I ought to do. I ought to realize that retirement didn't really change me all that much. I still have a bad case of the oughts. Middle age-plus or not, I ought to quit fooling myself. I won't really miss many of the meetings I ought to attend.

Even if I "ought" to.

Just Do It

Last Saturday I was responsible for several different activities around town as well as some personal duties that were time consuming. I was feeling overwhelmed by all that was facing me and commented to my husband that I would really be glad when this day was over. Instantly, I could hear, in memory, my mother's voice saying, "Don't wish your life away."

This started me thinking about all the sayings that we use to guide our lives or the lives of those around us. A very common one in my childhood home was "What will the neighbors think?" Many exciting plans of my youth were squelched with that one phrase.

It didn't matter that I didn't care what the neighbors thought. My mother obviously did, so our behavior was modified to meet what she felt the neighbors would approve.

Another standby, this time from my father, was "It'll be better by the time you are married." He used this for scraped knees, hurt feelings, or pouting sessions. The fact that it made no sense didn't seem to matter. We knew he meant to quit bellyaching (another favorite phrase of his) and go on with our life.

My husband's mother frequently used the phrase "You don't pay for your own raising until you have children of your own." She used that when telling a tale about her children as well as to us when we were struggling with our own household. We knew very well what she meant.

May Kennedy McCord, a radio personality in the Ozarks, used to end her programs with "I'll be back at this same time next week, Lord willin' and the crick don't rise." That has become a well used phrase in our home ever since I first heard it as a young bride.

More recent sayings often have their origin from a commercial or from a television star. "How sweet it is" by Jackie Gleason was used frequently several years ago and still hits home. "Just do it" started with a commercial in the 1990s and still is heard in many homes. In fact, I find myself urging myself on with that phrase when I am caught up in busyness as I was last Saturday.

"I can't believe I ate the whole thing!" "Where's the beef?" and "Please, Mother, I'd rather do it myself" have all become household phrases in the past decades and remain in many homes today. (That is one great thing about being this age. You can bring out an oldie and your grandchildren think it's great because they haven't heard it before.)

But I am trying very hard not to control the actions of those I love by sayings of a commercial or a television star. And I don't want to use trite sayings as guides to good living. No, I've been there, done that, got a tee shirt.

Is Small Beautiful?

I have a book entitled *Small Is Beautiful.* It is a book about economics as if people mattered. Recently, this book was mentioned in one of our Advent Sunday School lessons as an example of how small things, such as the birth of a baby, can be the most important thing in life. This past Christmas season has made me even more aware of the truth of this title.

Small towns are beautiful. Small churches are beautiful. Small children are beautiful. And small ideas can develop into very big things when the idea is beautiful.

A local columnist wrote recently about the joys she found shopping here in Nevada after facing the malls elsewhere. I echo that completely. Although I do much of my shopping by ordering, I do it through our own JC Penney outlet. The service at the local store makes the process comfortable, even when dealing with a large corporation.

On the weekend before Christmas, our refrigerator suddenly died. We discovered this about noon on Saturday. Though no repairmen could come at that time, three different stores on the square offered to remain open later than their usual hours if we wanted to buy a new refrigerator (which had been a halfway plan for Christmas anyway). When we made our selection, a salesman extended his day to deliver and help set up the box in our rural home so that we wouldn't have to be without refrigeration over the weekend. I doubt that could have been accomplished in a larger store or in a larger town. (The next week a repairman did come, and we now have an extra refrigerator in our breezeway—something we have needed for years—to help when our large family comes home.)

The Christmas activities in the county have been plentiful and varied, from fun to cultural. (Wait a minute. Culture can be fun, too!) A concert by local people may not have the musical merits of the Mormon Tabernacle Choir, but it is just as enjoyable to watch your neighbor, co-worker, or teacher singing as it is to hear the more trained voices who sing professionally.

Since Lester is now an Interim Minister at Moundville, Bronaugh, and Sheldon United Methodist Churches, we have been blessed by attending Christmas programs in these smaller churches. The smallest child who can stand is included, if just to shake some jingle bells. Three grade school boys sang "We Three Kings" in front of a full church of beaming adults. Some were parents or grandparents or other relatives. Regardless of blood relation or not, everyone present shared the pride and joy of youngsters willing to participate in the ancient pageant.

I couldn't help thinking that some children

in bigger communities have never felt this loving support and appreciation from a community. We took our great-granddaughter to see Santa come in on the train. This extra thrill of children who were not experienced in being near trains was a donation from the train company, and all the personnel on board were volunteering their time. Although our little one didn't win the electric train donated by the Sonic Drive-In, we were appreciative that a local business had added this extra excitement to the day.

The recent rash of takeovers to make businesses bigger and bigger has made many of us pull back. We still want to do business with a Sue in Nevada and not a Mr. Jones in Cincinnati who doesn't know or care about us. Although I respect and like the local personnel in these bigger corporations, I find myself drifting to the smaller Mom and Pop type business whenever possible. It is great to walk into a store and have someone tell me they remember my father or mother or maybe an older sibling. It is wonderful to sit in church with the lawyer who helped with a legal problem or the doctor who delivered our great-grandchild. And the delight of that same great-grandchild when she saw her preschool teacher in church was the highlight of our day.

So I agree small is beautiful. But as I write this article with the book on the table in front of me, I notice a small insert on the front which reads "More than 700,000 copies sold." Maybe in sales not all things small are beautiful!

If Cows Could Drive

I remarked to my husband recently that cows never seem to look up. They graze with their eyes to the ground. They drink their water in the same position. When they rest, they usually have their heads either at a level position or tilted slightly downward. They miss many of the things about this great world. They do not see the treetops, birds flying, or even the moon and stars, unless they see them reflected in the water of the pond they drink from. Cows seem to be content with their line of vision and rarely change it, except to look across the fence to see a commotion made by other animals or to watch for the truck bringing their supper of hay.

I heard that Lester used this thought as a sermon illustration after my remark. I wasn't there to hear it, so I don't know if he drew the same conclusions that I am writing now. We'll see.

Unlike cattle, we humans look in any direction we choose. We can see all the wonders skyward as well as the minute things under our feet. We can gaze into the distance or study something close at hand. There is very little that is out of our line of vision. But do we use this gift? Often we, like the cows, are zeroed in to opportunities for food, drink, or rest instead of looking around at other things.

This week I was driving down Austin Street when I noticed an older woman walking down the sidewalk. She was nearly bent double, probably by osteoporosis, but she was still walking quite briskly. She never took her eyes off the sidewalk, even though she passed by a beautiful blooming rosebush in the nearby lawn. I am sure she was being careful to watch her footing, so she wouldn't fall on a crack in the sidewalk, but it seemed a shame that she missed the beauty of the roses. I wondered how she kept a safe footing and still was able to enjoy her surroundings. The answer was clear. She could stop walking from time to time and look around to see what she was missing. Then she could continue her onward journey with head bent.

I hoped that when she reached her destination, she would be able to sit and rest for a while, maybe with her feet up. But I couldn't ponder her habits long because the traffic was thick on Austin Street that day, and the cruisers were making their presence felt. I had to watch my driving. I heard a friendly toot of a horn, but I couldn't look to see if a friend was greeting me or if it was for another driver. I had to watch my driving.

From the corner of my eye, I thought I saw two squirrels chasing each other up a tree, but I couldn't be sure. As I neared the west end of the street, I saw people on Cottey College campus with something in the air that looked like balloons or a kite. Since Cottey's term was over for the year, I was curious about what was happening. But I couldn't really tell. I had to watch my driving.

After I left the city limits, the traffic let up somewhat, but I was hurrying to get home to make a phone call. I drove at the speed limit to get home quickly. I didn't notice much about my surroundings except to realize that the blackberries were in bloom. Or maybe it was multiflora rose. I couldn't tell for sure. I had to watch my speedier driving.

As I turned onto our county road, I did notice how tall the weeds had grown but saw that our good neighbor had mowed one swath on the road by our property. I couldn't see much of it because I met another car going fast, and I couldn't see through the cloud of dust he stirred up. I really had to watch my driving in that condition.

When I arrived home, I made my phone call and then went outside to relax in the lawn a moment. Up the driveway, I could see Dorothy Tyer's cows grazing in their lane with their heads to the ground. I gave a prayer of thanks that I wasn't a cow.

If I had been a cow, I wouldn't have been able to drive. Think what I would have missed seeing!

Why?

I think I have found one of the bonds between grandparents and grandchildren or great-grandchildren. It is the desire to ask why.

Our great-granddaughters are all at the age where the most persistent question they ask is why? A recent conversation is an example.

"What are you doing, Grandmommy?"

"I am getting ready to go to town."

"Why?"

"Because I have a meeting to go to."

"Why?"

So I ponder the question. Why am I going? Because I am on the committee is my answer. But then her question remains. Why? I have to admit to myself that I like being on committees that make decisions about important things.

But then the memory of her question comes back. Why? Because I want to feel important? Because I want to be in on things that are happening? Because I like to be with people who are interested in things I am also interested in? Because I was raised by parents who were very involved in things in the community? And because I haven't learned to say no.

But why?

I haven't learned to say no because I really don't want to say no. Not yet. Some things I can say no to very easily. I can say no to most telephone solicitors. I can say no to these same great-granddaughters when they want the third piece of candy before dinner. And I can say no to many temptations to indulge myself. But I don't say no to requests that seem to need my talents. Maybe I am still trying to prove that I have talents.

Why?

Our generation has the freedom to ask why more often than when we were caught up in all the activities of job and family. In those days, we rushed through the hours doing what had to be done without question. Now there is a *little* more time to question the necessity of some things. For instance, we always have a big dinner at noon on Sundays.

Why?

Sometimes we can have sandwiches even if it is Sunday. When we get an early morning call while we are still in bed, we always deny that the call woke us up.

Why?

We have a right to sleep in if our own schedules permit it. Or if we spend the whole evening watching silly sitcoms on television, we insist that we were really reading the paper and the tube just happened to be on.

Why?

What's in the paper probably isn't any more enlightening than the comedies.

So we middle age-plus folks can come into

our second childhood with this child-like ability to question. We can ignore some of the customs and habits of the past after putting them to the why test. Things that seemed important don't always remain so if we ask the why question.

But why?

As I am answering the fifteenth query from one of my littlest relatives, I try not to become annoyed and be thankful that her mind is sorting out things that are important. I can realize that the "Why?" stage is a natural part of growing up.

And now it seems it is becoming a natural part of growing old.

I wonder why?

The Damage Is Done

A television program I was watching recently said that people who have wrinkles and brown spots on their faces caused this problem by too much exposure to the sun when they were children or teenagers. The damage done then waited until this age to show up. Another program explained that many of our fat cells were developed in early life and predisposed us to being overweight in adulthood.

Then, just yesterday, I heard on the news that the damage done to our ear canals by listening to loud music or being around noisy machinery as we were growing up could hasten the condition we call "hard of hearing."

So here we are, middle age-plus, with wrinkled skin, fat tummies, and poor hearing, and it all happened before we knew any better. I see two ways to respond to this dilemma. We can decide that it doesn't matter anymore because the damage is already done. Therefore, we can pig out while sitting in the sun and listening to music on our ghetto blaster. Or we can give up watching television programs and reading material that explains the mess we're in. If we don't know, then we can still fool ourselves that someday we really will lose those ten (twenty?) pounds, find a cream that removes our wrinkles, and get the wax out of our ears. We can pretend that we still have some control over these aging bodies.

The only other solution is one we know won't work because our parents tried it on us. That is to get our kids and grandkids to quit doing these things that bring on some aging problems.

We all know that those under twenty-five never see themselves having the unpleasant symptoms of aging. They hope to grow to be very old, but they also KNOW that they will never lose control of any of their bodily functions. They will waltz into old age with vim and vigor as agile, graceful, and coordinated as they are in their youth.

I doubt we will get very far convincing them to cover their skin, tone down their music, or cut back on the French fries. We didn't, so why should they? Unless, maybe, this new generation is smarter than we were, and they will heed our warnings? Nah!

So let's go back to our first solution. Quit worrying. Enjoy life. The damage is done. We have some defects from age, but hey, we can still have fun. Just keep the doctor's number handy and live it up in spite of what we did to ourselves when we were young and ignorant. Now we are a little older, a little smarter, not as pretty or as athletic, but we still know how to have a good time. Grab your hearing aids and let's party!

"The Missus" Buys a Tractor

Recently we had occasion to make a rather expensive purchase. (Expensive for us, that is.) Because costs of this amount are not usual for us, we spent a long time looking over the options and comparing quality, costs, and how well the item met our needs. One thing we did not compare, but which probably had a bigger effect than we realized, was the attitude of the sales people.

On one of our shopping days, we were each in town in different vehicles. I arrived at the first store several minutes before Lester. I looked over the possibilities, read the attached tags, and even sat in the seat of several of the tractors we were considering. No one paid any attention to me. Two salesmen walked through the show room but didn't stop to ask if they could help. Finally, just minutes before Lester arrived, I was waited on. However, as soon as my husband walked inside, the attention transferred to him. To make matters worse, the salesman referred to me as, "The Missus".

At another stop, we arrived together, and the conversation was again directed to Lester.

At the third store, the salesman introduced himself, asked our names (both of us), shook hands with each of us, and continued to divide his information and time equally between us. (The fact that he told me that he read my columns didn't hurt my feelings, either!)

It turned out that we made our purchase at this third store. I think we really preferred this tractor to the others, but I also believe that our (my) treatment entered into the decision.

This experience reminded me of other instances when I did or did not buy something due to my feelings about how I was treated. Now that I am middle age-plus, I notice more condescending attitudes from some sales people. I don't like to be called "Darling." At one place where I traded, the salesman used this term regularly. I asked my younger friends if he ever called them "Darling." None had that experience; however, other older women had. I know the man was just trying to be nice to us little old ladies, but I wasn't his darling no matter what my age.

Recently, I received a telephone solicitation wanting to send a free book for my child between the ages of three and eight. I told the young lady that I was past having a child of that age. Her tone immediately changed to almost baby talk while she tried to persuade me that I probably had grandchildren then, didn't I, and wouldn't they love to have a book from good old grandma. I didn't take the bait and wouldn't have even if she addressed me as if I had good sense. I know I may be over reacting to well meaning attitudes, but that's part of the fun of being middle age-plus. You have already established your reputations, so you can go ahead and react if you want to.

It's okay, "Darling."

I Just Love...

If you are middle age-plus, I can wager that when you were growing up you didn't hear the words "I love you" very often, especially out in public. I have never for a minute doubted that I was loved by my parents and my family (well, most of the time), but I don't remember ever hearing any one of them tell me "I love you." And I didn't tell them that either, even though I thought my brothers and sisters were the cutest, best-looking, and smartest of all the young people I knew.

We didn't go around saying those three little words. I also don't remember hearing either of my parents saying them to each other. I often saw them kiss, hold hands, and certainly smile those knowing smiles of parents. But I didn't hear them express their love in words.

Our children, grandchildren, and certainly our great-granddaughters tell us quite often that they love us. It sounds good, and I am glad they can easily express their feelings. However, one little one uses it almost as a weapon. When she thinks we are disappointed in something she has done, she beats us to the punch with, "I love you, Grandmommy." It's hard to chastise someone after that greeting.

We use the word *love* freely in everyday conversation. "I love bananas." "I just loved that book." Or, "I love what you have done to your hair." Maybe we have taken away some of the emotions of the word with this casual usage so that it comes easier to say to other people.

I have even heard *love* used in connection with its opposite, *hate.* Such as "I'd love to see that old so and so get what's coming to him" or "I'd love to see her face when she hears about what happened."

Songs about love are plentiful. Some use the broader meaning of the word. "I love New York in June, how about you?" Others get to the heart very quickly. "I'm in the Mood for Love," and "Love's Old Sweet Song." I suppose some of the newer songs are also about love, but since I can't understand the words, I can't really be sure. I have the feeling that some of them are more about passion than love, but then you must remember that I am the official old fogey. I could be wrong.

I think the English-Scottish trait of being reserved accounts for much of the lack of expressed emotion in my generation of my family. If I came from a different heritage, I might be expressing completely different ideas. We were supposed to be stiff-lipped and proper. We didn't raise our voices in anger or get away with crying or sulking. When I heard an argument among adults in another house, I ran home thinking the family was near a breakdown. But the next morning they came by smiling and waving as if nothing had happened.

My heritage, however, never got in the way when I was with my husband-to-be. Words came quite easily there and even were expressed on paper when he was in the service. Now they are expressed more by actions than words. An offer to eat supper out when I've had a hard day can say more than many words. Or a shoulder to lean on when things aren't going well says volumes. Love of country, love of home, love of animals and nature, all add to the feeling of well-being that lives in those who are loved and can love others. I can't imagine life without love, and I am very grateful to my parents, who didn't say the words, but showed me in every way that they did love me.

I'd love to write more about this, but I also love my sleep, and it's getting late.

So till next time, Love ya!

Stuff

Do you ever wonder what will happen to all your stuff when you die? Every time I clean house I think that I really should get rid of some of this stuff. I start to sort through my treasurers and spend hours rereading letters and looking at pictures and church and club materials. I end up with only one wastebasket's worth to throw away. But I have had a nice time in memory land.

Many of us have experienced the sad duty of disposing of possessions where a loved one has died. Some things can be handled quickly because of the obvious economic or legal actions needed. But the little things that had been put on the back of the shelves or the letters stuck back in a drawer are more difficult. The sentiment attached to them makes it hard to toss them coldly in the trash. Also we each remember wishing we had held on to some discarded possession when it became valuable through time.

I decided that I would save my sister Miriam's books, knick-knacks, and small things to let anyone in our large family choose items they wanted while they were at our family reunion. They did take quite a few things, but since many were flying, they couldn't take everything. We then had to decide what to do with the remaining things and were happy that the library and college took her books.

Now I am looking at things in our house. Who would ever want all this stuff? We should have cleaned out the stuff when we moved back here years ago, but since we didn't have time, we just moved it all and stored it until we had more time to go through it. It is still there. We haven't gone through it either carefully or hurriedly.

I've heard that if you haven't used something in three years, you should get rid of it. But in the process of gathering it up to throw out or get rid of, you realize how interesting, pretty, valuable, meaningful all this stuff is, so you want to keep it. Anyway, who knows what child or grandchild might want these items for emotional or historic value?

Once while cleaning house so that our own family (fifteen people and two dogs) could stay with us during the reunion, our daughter-in-law threw out some stuff and moved other things. We really appreciated her help, but I'm still looking for one or two things which hopefully weren't thrown away. I know that hot pad had a burned hole and was frayed on one side, but I liked the way it fit the pans. And the knife with the loose handle was going to be fixed as soon as we got around to it.

We always believe there will be more time to do some of these things next winter or next year when we finish this project or responsibility. Then we always manage to take on more jobs that are more fun than going through all our stuff.

We did gather up a trailer load of broken machinery and tools to take in for resale. After two days of work, we received the magnificent sum of $12.43 for the scrap metal. But at least we got rid of some stuff that can be used again.

If I leave a lot of my stuff for the next generation to dispose of, maybe some of it will be recycled. Wouldn't that be better than my throwing it away now?

I'm all for recycling, especially if we can recycle stuff to the next generation.

I Am Happy with the Way Things Look

I like to mow the lawn. It is great to look back and see what I have accomplished and know that I have made a difference by my work.

Getting older is somewhat like that. I can look back and see the path I have made through life and know that, at times, I really have made a difference. It isn't always easy to realize that my actions are very important. But as time goes on and I look back, I can see how I have influenced others. For example, when I look back on my childhood as the youngest child of a big family, I realize what a difference I made to my siblings.

My family grew up knowing about parenting and child care by taking care of me. In fact, to hear most of them talk, you would think my mother did nothing but sit and rock while they did all the child care and housework!

I was the perfect teacher for them with my whining to go with a brother when he went to pick up his date, crying that if someone didn't take me to the library *that night* all my books would be over-due, and we would be broke paying all the fines and, finally, speaking up at the dinner table about what I had seen in their closets. Yes, I really made a big difference in my family. Maybe that is why one sister never had any children!

In my early married years, I made my mark by instructing my husband in the proper type of gravy to have with meals and the fun of over-spending at Christmastime.

Later years had me sharing this influence on my own children as I convinced them that taking band made more sense than playing football and that no one really noticed what kind of shoes they were wearing. Now with a trumpet tarnishing in the closet, my son spends every weekend coaching Little League or watching sports on television. I really made a difference. But now he is also telling his sons that no one really notices what kind of shoes they're wearing.

So here I am in my mature years. I don't have to worry about my influence anymore. Like the lawn I am mowing, the path is already cut, and I can't do anything except wait for time to cover up the marks. If I did hit a few molehills, scalp a few high spots, or leave some tall grass in the corner, it won't really matter in the long run. In a little while no one will know.

And really when I look back, I am pretty happy with the way things look.

But you also must remember that my eyesight isn't quite as good as it used to be!

5

Time Out
Past Time
and
Recreation

*For when I was a babe and wept and slept,
Time crept, When I was a boy and laughed and
talked, Time walked; Then when the years saw
me a man, Time ran, But as I older grew, Time
flew.*

*inscribed on a clock in Chester
cathedral by Guy Pentreath*

Sinful Games

My brother Ralph lives in a retirement village. This facility has opportunities for recreation right on the grounds, so within a few steps he can find entertainment and companionship. But he has a severe handicap in taking advantage of one of the most popular recreations. He had never played pool before he moved there. Most of the other residents grew up playing pool and beat the socks off him when he first tried to compete.

Ralph was skilled at various sports, including basketball, volleyball, track, canoeing, and hiking, but he had not played pool because he grew up in Nevada where our family, and other families like ours, looked upon playing pool as sinful. He told me that when my mother walked with him and his younger brother Vernon from the square down to Moore's Department Store to buy their new overalls for the year, she crossed the street to the north side so that my brothers could not look into the doors of the pool hall that was in the middle of the block on the south side. She did not want them to be exposed to such an environment, even from the street. I am sure there must have been very fine families in Nevada who had pool tables in their home, and perhaps the Country Club had pool tables there for their members. But the rural families in our neighborhood did not have this opportunity nor did they want it. The sport was an evil pastime that would lead to nothing good.

Later, my sister Ellen and I experienced a similar prejudice against what we considered a harmless, wholesome sport when we wanted to take bowling as our class for physical education when we were in high school and college. To our mother, bowling alleys were almost as bad as pool halls. She couldn't see why a nice school would expose the students to such an atmosphere. Since this was in Washington D.C. and was a different environment for her, she finally consented. We bowled many a line in a nearby bowling alley. I don't think I became any more sinful after the experience. At that stage in my life, meeting boys was my primary obsession, and I am sure that with my long skinny legs and awkwardness, I didn't attract many boys as I stumbled around the alleys. I did become a fair bowler though.

My husband grew up in a family that looked upon playing cards as sinful. They could play dominos, Rook, or Old Maid, but could not play anything with a poker deck. When Lester went to high school at the School of the Ozarks (which prohibited playing cards also), he learned to play cards and became quite good at it. His older sister found out that he had a deck of cards and took them away from him for fear he would be expelled. It didn't stop his card playing nor his education as he is now good at most card games and is also a respected minister. Perhaps his early sinfulness didn't hurt him too badly.

I look at some of the activities of the youngsters around me and wonder if these will also turn out to be as harmless as playing pool, bowling, or playing cards were to our generation.

If you're looking for a really sinful game, I think perhaps the old familiar Old Maid is one of the worst. It characterizes and ridicules a whole group of people who have added much to our society throughout the years.

But no one wants to be left with the Old Maid. Now that's sinful!

Skinned Knees and Smashed Thumbs

Every year as school starts again, I get nostalgic for my roller skates. When I was a child in Washington, D.C., my sister and I, with neighbor kids, skated the mile to our grade school. Most of the children in the school were not well dressed unless they wore a skate key around their neck and carried or wore a pair of skates.

These metal wheeled skates were fastened to our shoes at the toe with clamps tightened with the key and at the heel with a leather strap. Today's children could not use this type of skate because the shoes they wear don't have heavy soles that protrude beyond the leather upper part of the shoe.

But in the days of our childhood, shoe skates were rare. We all had the clamp-on kind. We skated down the sidewalks, jumped the curbs into the street at crossings, and got to school in a hurry. At school, we removed our skates, put them in the cloakroom, and waited until the three o'clock bell to put them back on. Going home, we didn't always take the quickest route but searched for hills and wide sidewalks to add to our fun.

Occasionally, a skate jiggled loose at the clasp, and one of us tumbled down as we lost a skate. Skinned knees and even smashed thumbs were common when we tried a new maneuver or hit a pebble that threw us down. Mishaps like this didn't stop us for long, unless we had to walk home carrying a broken skate. Since new skates were hard to come by, a real accident that ruined a skate was a catastrophe. However, we skated on one skate and used the other foot to add speed, as if we were using a scooter.

In summer, in Nevada, we always looked forward to the temporary wooden-floored skating rink under a tent. The sides were open air but had screens or chicken wire to keep nonpaying people out. Our parents sat in cars surrounding the rink and listened to the music and watched us go round and round in front of them. We rented shoe skates with softer wheels at the rink.

It was a fun, cool way to spend an evening, and the older people enjoyed visiting outside while we skated.

When our children were small, we went to neighboring Ft. Scott to skate at an upstairs rink. This more permanent rink had a composition floor that was steadier than the temporary wooden one in the tent. We did the usual games at the rink, such as the limbo and looby-loo, while enjoying community fun. Often we had a 4-H skating party or just a group of neighbors went together. Even though this was intended for children, many of us adults got on the floor.

(Some literally did get ON the floor!)

I taught three of our older grandchildren to skate in a rink in Independence, Missouri, where we often went with church youth groups. It has been several years since I actually skated, but I would still enjoy it. It may not be the smartest thing for me to do, but I've never been known for brains anyway.

When I see our local students getting on the school buses, I feel sorry for them that they don't have the fun of clamping on a pair of sidewalk skates and heading to school in style.

Dribbling Memories

I've had a great time this week reliving my basketball-playing memories. Thanks to a call from one of our athletes wanting information on girls' basketball, I got started on a whole new subject for an article.

I didn't go to Nevada High School, and when my older sisters went there, the sport was not played. Girls and boys that lived in the country had trouble being in any extracurricular activities anyway because of transportation problems. But I did play intramural basketball at Woodrow Wilson High School in Washington, D.C.

When I first started playing, the court was divided into six sections, with a girl from each team in each of these sections. The idea was that girls should not run the full length of the court because of some imagined weakness in our gender. Therefore, we did a lot of just grabbing the ball and wildly throwing it to the forwards on the other side of the line. They could try to make a basket. Since I was taller than most of my friends, as guard, I spent my basketball days thrashing my arms about over the head of some poor little forward who usually maneuvered around me easily.

Another concession to our gender was that we could bounce the ball only once. There was no practiced skill of dribbling the ball. It was jump up to catch the ball, and then throw it to another player while trying to keep the one girl in your section from making a basket.

The girls' gym at this brand new school had no provision for audiences, except for a few feet on either side of the playing court. There was a balcony above, where the gym teachers had their offices, and sometimes folding chairs could be placed there for someone to watch below. But the playing was mainly done for our own enjoyment. We never played with another school's team. I don't think even the boys played many games with other schools.

The boys' gym was down the hall from ours. We weren't supposed to go there, but I did peek in once. It did not have any seating arrangements either, so if the boys played other teams, it wasn't as a spectator sport. This was wartime and restrictions on using cars for nonessential reasons eliminated many competitions. Also this city school had no buses to transport players to another school. However, the football teams did play other schools but only in the afternoon because of the prohibition of using lights at night.

It is probably just as well that there were no audiences at these games since our green gym suits weren't too flattering. They were one piece uniforms with built-in bloomers under a short pleated skirt. The top was shirtwaist style with one pocket, a collar, and a zipper in the front.

We had lockers in the dressing room for storing this suit, our gym shoes, socks, and a towel to use after our mandatory showers, which we never took. I think we took the whole outfit home to wash once or twice each semester, but I can't really remember doing that. I do remember the odor in the dressing room.

Before graduating from high school, we played on half the court but couldn't cross the line. A typical game had girls standing at the center line frantically catching or throwing the ball to the other side and maybe one or two smarter players back under the basket waiting for a lobbed ball to come their way. We had very little coaching, so size and energy usually won over strategy.

When our children played basketball in Missouri, girls used the same rules as boys. They ran the full distance of the court and dribbled the ball up and down the floor. I don't think our daughter, who played varsity basketball and indulged in all that running, suffered a bit from the activity. In fact, I know she is healthier than I was at her age. And I know she looked better in her uniform than I did. In spite of all the restrictions, basketball was one of my favorite sports. From the enthusiasm I feel from my middle age-plus friends here in the county who were able to have a team, I think my feelings are reflected by many of *the weaker sex.*

Play Ball!

Take me out to the ball game—to enjoy the dust, the hard seats on the bleachers, and the heat. We also enjoy the friendship of shared interest in our children and grandchildren and enjoy participating in the community spirit as we cheer for our home team and catch up on local news.

Recently, we drove to Butler to watch two of our grandsons Michael and Les play in two different games back to back. The ballfields had four different lighted diamonds, all in use. Similar activities happen in our town each night and in most other cities across the nation. These games replace to some extent the over-the-fence neighborliness and visiting of earlier days while giving our youngster training in sports and in community involvement.

As we drove home, I reminisced about the ball fields of my youth. At an intersection of Highways 54 and 43 near us, simply known as the Corner, Dan Todd set aside some of his land for a ball diamond, complete with backstop and a bench for spectators. Here all the neighborhood kids gathered for games of work-up practice as teams and some competitive play with other teams. Across the road was The Station, a garish green building with gas pumps outside and inside a wealth of rare treats for the kids who gathered for the games.

This was the first place I ever drank soda pop from a bottle. A commercial container with hinged doors on top held a large chunk of ice and various varieties of pop in tall glass bottles. We had the fun of fishing through the icy water with our hands to find the flavor we wanted. The bottles were so big that my friend Joyce and I shared one five-cent bottle and spent another nickel on a huge candy bar we shared with several friends.

As we got older, we became part of the girls' softball team which broke customs of the time by choosing pants to play in. Actually, they were blue and white striped bib overalls such as the local farmers wore to work. Dan Todd's daughter Agnes was the pitcher, Joyce was short stop, Ellen was third base, the Maple girls, the Taylors, the Phelps, and others in the neighborhood filled other positions.

I was substitute centerfield; that tells much about my ball playing abilities! I stood far out, hoping and praying that no ball ever reached me.

At that time, I was growing rapidly, and it seemed each time I bent over to get a ground ball, the ground was a half inch lower. At least I missed many balls by about that distance. Fly balls were even worse. As we played most games at twilight and center field faced west, the balls got lost in the sun and then thumped down beside me before I even spotted them. A good day for me was when I wasn't needed and could sit on the bench to cheer the team on.

Today this field is part of the right-of-way where the four-lane highway ends. Often as I pass, I still look for that ugly green station and a field of young people having fun together while their parents and neighbors watch.

Middle age-plus folks don't play excellent ball, but our memories can outlast all aches and pains.

Saturday Nights

I was tired Saturday night after cleaning
house and catching up after a busy week. I settled
in our lounge chair, had a cold drink at my elbow,
the remote control for the television in my hand,
and the Sunday School lesson nearby in case I
felt like reviewing it again. Then I thought, this
is Saturday night. This is the special night of the
week for kicking up your heels. I looked at my
heels which were at eye level at this point and
decided I really was getting older because I had
no desire to go anywhere else. If I kicked up my
heels at all, it would be to elevate the chair a bit
more so I could even take a slight snooze.

Memories of past Saturday nights began to
take the place of the drama unfolding on the
screen. I remember those agonizing Saturday
nights when I was a teenager and did not have a
date. I wouldn't put my nose out the door for
fear I'd be seen and the whole world would know
that I did not have a date! (Who says the teen
years are the happiest of your life?)

But then there were the Saturday nights when
I did have a date. We would go to the dance hall

on the island at Radio Spring Park and dance to the juke box or once in a great while to a live band. Afterwards, we would go up on the square and get curb service outside Wiggs' Drug Store and watch people around the square. We didn't know the term cruising, but the square was where everyone congregated and drove around and around to find a parking place or just to see and be seen.

In those wonderful years before dating age, the square on Saturday night was an exciting meeting place for special people. My friend Joyce and I spent hours selecting the very best buys of candy at the Kress dime store on the west side. After making that selection, we would see if we had enough money to buy a bag of popcorn at the stand at the bottom of a stairway in the middle of the west side of the square or at the little cart at the northwest corner. If we stayed long enough to get hungry again, we'd go down to Ratts' Brothers Creamery to get a double-dip cone for a nickel. We did all of this for a dime apiece, if we shared.

The very best part of those Saturday nights was making our way around the square dressed up in our nicest clothes. We saw everyone we knew and enjoyed being part of an exciting mixture of Vernon County residents. It often took half an hour to cover just one or two sides of the square because of the crowds and the fun of visiting.

I can't forget the Saturday night neighborhood square dances we held in each other's home with the Johnson boys furnishing the music and sometimes calling the dances. The parents came to watch and often dance. The little kids ran and played Flying Dutchman or Two Deep while the older kids danced. Wash tubs of ice filled with bottled soft drinks furnished the only refreshments, but no one seemed to mind.

So here I am with my soft drink, in my comfortable chair, enjoying the memories. I do *not* feel like the old song "Saturday Night Is the Loneliest Night of the Week." I can enjoy the memories of Saturdays past without wishing them back.

I like it this way.

In the Swim

I'd like to go swimming today. It's hot and the water looks inviting. Since I have become middle age-plus, I find it takes more courage to go swimming. It's not that I am afraid of the water. I am afraid of my bathing suit! Somehow those suits that look so nice in the catalog lose some of their appeal when I wear them. If I could just immediately get in the water before anyone sees me, then I'd be fine. Underwater I look okay.

One great thing about our home is that we have possibilities for private swimming in our pond. I usually swim in whatever shorts I have been working in. I don't even have to use that pretty bathing suit. But because it is a pond (even though we have given it a sand floor where we enter), whatever we wear must have the pond water washed off very soon.

This pond wasn't created when I was a child. Then we had other places where we enjoyed the cooling fun of swimming. My earliest memories of swimming were in Radio Springs Lake in Nevada. As I remember it, there was a roped-off area right in front of the bathhouse. That bathhouse had wide cracks in the floor where I could see the lake beneath my feet while I changed clothes. I think there was a shower inside the ladies' side, but I can't picture it clearly. The lake had a long sliding board in the water which must have been a little rustic because one time it tore a big hole in the seat of my sister's bathing suit. She wouldn't get out of the water until we got her a towel.

As all youth like to do, we enjoyed going out of town to swim and for other recreation. The pool at Ft. Scott was exciting for us because of its size and its sliding board with two hills that gave an extra zip to the slide.

I recall that these bathhouses had showers between each dressing stall where we often washed our hair because we didn't have that facility at home.

Later, Nevada had a swimming pool built in the lake at Radio Springs Park. It still used the same old bathhouse. I imagined the same old spiders watching me from beneath the cracks in the floor.

Some of my favorite swimming places were not in pools but in more natural settings. I was a grown woman before I knew that the term "strip pits" referred to a type of mining that produced the dangerous swimming places down near Moundville. I thought the term referred to the type of swimming done there!

Another favorite was the asphalt pit near our farm. This was the scene of many a watermelon-eating, swimming party for area youth. The dressing facilities were behind bushes or the back seat of a car. Though the floor of the pit had rocks and other obstacles, we still enjoyed moonlight swims on hot summer nights after the work was done.

Safer places to swim are now available in our area, and we can be proud of the opportunities we have for water sport. But none can be any more fun than those cooling spots of my youth.

Let's Go to the Movies

I grew up going to the movies at least once or twice a week. I clearly remember being unimpressed with the first talkie when my parents took me to see Al Jolson. I went to sleep in my mother's lap and asked her to wake me up when the blankets came down. I liked the stage show much better. That soon changed, and I became an avid fan.

I remember an older sister Gertrude walking with Ellen and me to the Avalon Theater on Connecticut Avenue in Washington, D.C. We saw *39 Steps*. I didn't understand all of this mystery plot, but Gertrude explained it as we walked home. (There was never any hesitation in our neighborhood to walk anywhere at any time of the day or night.) I watched this movie recently and again cherished the memory of a big sister taking the time to let her two younger sisters enjoy a classic with her.

With this long history of attending movies, I feel like a has-been when I watch the award shows. They show beautiful young people who starred in a movie I never heard of. What's more, I haven't heard of half of the beautiful young actors. I know I am getting to be an old fogey, but it seems like we are so bombarded with personalities these days that very few really catch our attention for long.

When I was young (this statement should be accompanied by my looking over the top of my glasses, but you can't see me, so I will leave them comfortably where they are), everybody knew Clark Gable, Jimmy Stewart, and Bette Davis, even if they didn't go to a lot of movies.

If I start listing some of the stars today that I do recognize, you will recognize a pattern rather quickly. Many of them share middle age-plus with me, most have been in movies and/or television for several years, and most will be in shows that have only a small group of regulars.

Some shows have so many characters and so many subplots that I can't get interested in watching week after week. And dare I confess that sometimes all those good-looking young men look so much alike to me that I can't distinguish the characters? I don't expect all the good guys to wear white hats, but at the end of the show, I'd like to know who the good guys are.

I can recognize the women better because of their hair styles and clothing. On *ER* I don't confuse the Hispanic nurse with all that abundant black, curly hair with the new doctor intern with the straight blond hair. But you notice I'm not using the names of either of the actresses because I don't know them without looking them up in *TV Guide*. Even there the writers often do not give the name of the regulars, identifying only the guest stars.

For someone who sometimes has trouble remembering the names of my life-long neighbors, I really have trouble remembering these stars that glitter so brightly for a short while on our screens.

But I always know Dick Van Dyke, Katherine Hepburn, Andy Griffith, and Bill Cosby. Maybe when our new multi-plex theater opens, they could have a section where they show only old-time films. Maybe some of our kids and grandkids would actually enjoy them. But we might have to explain when the camera moves from a couple in love to a view out the window that they are to use their imagination for what is going on. It won't be portrayed on the screen in living, breathing, panting color!

Basket Dinners

I am sitting in my house wearing two sweaters, looking out at several inches of snow in near zero temperature. So what am I thinking about? I am remembering those wonderful community basket dinners that we used to have every summer in the shade of big elm trees.

Those events were exciting to me because all the neighbors came which meant I had lots of children to play with. I even enjoyed the preparations when the dinners were held at our house. We put some new two-by-twelve boards across a series of saw horses to form one very long table for the food. We arranged a shorter table for the big container of iced tea. I suppose there was coffee, but since that didn't interest me, I can't remember.

We covered the boards with newly washed and bleached sheets which we tucked in under the boards to keep the ever-present southwest wind from causing havoc. The neighbors brought big baskets of food and their own plates, silver, and cups. I have no memory of any napkins, but I suppose, if any were used, they were brought by each family. This was before paper napkins, cups, and plates.

I remember what seemed like miles of platters

of fried chicken, pots of green beans, corn, and peas with potatoes. Salads were mostly slaw, applesauce, and jello, if the weather was cool enough to keep it firm. I don't remember raw vegetables such as carrot sticks, celery, and certainly not broccoli or cauliflower. If raw vegetables were there, I would have ignored them, as I usually grabbed a drumstick and then headed for the desserts.

Although my mother was a great cook, making wonderful cakes and pies, I enjoyed all those other goodies our neighbors brought. I could always count on a slice of angelfood cake or a piece of cherry pie.

Part of our preparations ahead of time was providing seating arrangements for some older neighbors. To supplement our wooden lawn chairs and every chair in the house that we carried outside, we placed boards across kitchen chairs to accommodate several people at once. No one had folding lawn chairs. Most of us sat on the grass, the steps, or some sat on the bumpers or running boards of their cars.

After eating, we kids played running and hiding games, teenagers gathered for conversation (or flirting), and adults sat in the shade and visited. One time I remember the adults went into the house to sing. My sister and I were shocked when a male quartet formed, and our father was one of the singers. We did not know that he ever sang in public, and we were astonished to hear how well he sang.

Hopefully, this present snow will soon melt. Until then, I will keep remembering those wonderful summers of my youth.

6

Did I Ever Tell You?
Reminiscing Life's
Experiences

*After the age of eighty, everything reminds
you of something else.*

Lowell Thomas in Time magazine

My Visit with Eleanor Roosevelt

Most people have fifteen minutes of glory sometime in their lives. I thought my fifteen minutes would happen in 1943 when Eleanor Roosevelt visited Woodrow Wilson High School in Washington, D.C.

My high school had such a large enrollment that all the students could not be in the auditorium at one time. For this occasion, they divided the student body. Half would be released from classes to line the curved drive that led from the street to the auditorium entrance. The other half would be seated in the auditorium.

In this high school, the pupils were assigned home rooms, which were then assigned to a house. Each house was named for an event in Woodrow Wilson's life. I was in Geneva House. You can imagine the excitement when it was announced over the intercom that Geneva House would be one of the groups allowed in the auditorium to hear the First Lady's talk.

My friends and I plotted our route to the auditorium to get there ahead of the other students. We had visions of being first-row-center when she arrived.

Two days before the big event, I was called to the principal's office with several other seniors. I wasn't nervous because I knew the principal fairly well and didn't think I was in any trouble. But I was very curious about what was happening.

To my surprise, when I arrived, I learned that he had chosen twenty student leaders to be on the stage when Mrs. Roosevelt made her speech. My astonishment at being considered one of the leaders of the school equaled my excitement at being that close to a famous person.

Living in the nation's capital, we were used to seeing motorcades on the city streets and catching glimpses of the President or a visiting dignitary from another country. I also had the fun of living as a neighbor to a pair of toddler twins who were godchildren of Mrs. Roosevelt. We often saw Mrs. Roosevelt driving her little coupe down the drive to visit the children. Usually she was alone in those pre-secret service days. Sometimes she was driven by her chauffeur but still in a small, ordinary coupe.

But this visit to the school was different. It would be filled with pomp and circumstance. She would actually be there for a half hour or more, and she was coming to see *us*.

My father was not a fan of the Roosevelts. When he heard the news, he suggested some ideas I might give the First Lady about how her husband was running the country.

My mother was concerned about what I wore, and my older sister kept telling me to keep my knees together when I was seated on the stage.

When the big day finally arrived, we were to

be in our places twenty minutes before her arrival. The outdoor students were jostling one another to be in the front row by the driveway; the indoor students rushed to the auditorium to get choice seats. With the nineteen other leaders who were to share the stage with me, I walked leisurely to the stage door entrance and on to my assigned seat on the stage. I was front row center after all—right behind the podium where I would have a choice look at the *back* of our First Lady!

We sat down and waited eagerly for the telltale cheer from outside that would alert us that Mrs. Roosevelt had arrived. Then we waited less eagerly. Finally, a half hour later we heard cheering outside, and we all stood as instructed to show respect and be able to see the procession more clearly.

One man preceded Mrs. Roosevelt up the aisle, then Mr. Nelson, our principal, walked beside her. That was the big procession. Our high school band played something patriotic as she was seated at the end of the first row of seats. Mr. Nelson introduced our guest. Mrs. Roosevelt stood, made a very short address about something, which I do not remember at all, then Mr. Nelson indicated that the stage was full of student leaders. Mrs. Roosevelt nodded in our direction and turned to leave.

I knew that her stocking seams were straight, that she was wearing the same type of old woman shoes that my mother wore, and that she was within five feet of where I was seated. But I never saw her face except in one fleeting glance as she was introduced to the school leaders.

Her exit was more hurried than her entrance. Within seconds, it seemed, she was gone. We heard another cheer from outside, and then the bell rang to return to classes.

We consoled ourselves that we would be mentioned in *My Day*, the daily column she wrote for the newspapers. When it came out the next day, the very last line in the column read, "I visited two schools today, one for the white and one for the colored."

So went my fifteen minutes of glory.

A Great Honor

I have received a few honors in my life that have made me feel good. But a recent honor has made me feel very special. I was elected president of the Ellis Domestic Science Club. This may not sound like much to the average person, but I consider it a great privilege. I will be serving as president of the club my mother started when the club reaches its 80th anniversary. Not many people have the opportunity to be a part of something started by their mother that is still going strong after eighty years.

In 1915, clubs for rural women were not common, but since my mother and a friend Josephine Gist wanted a club for their neighborhood, they organized the Ellis Domestic Science Club on September 22.

At that time, my mother had four children and was pregnant with the fifth. (*Pregnant* is a word my mother never would have said!) But in spite of the problems of a house full of kids, she and other women thought it would be good to get together twice a month for educational and social contacts.

It was, indeed, very good.

My mother was Pearl Gray, but she never identified herself that way. In her time, she was always Mrs. Chester H. Gray. The women in the club called one another Mrs. Kafer, Mrs. Todd, and Mrs. Taylor, never Elva, Maggie or Bertha.

Through the years, the club has been a prominent part of the Ellis community. The present members represent second and third generations of members. Dorothy Vohs was a member longer than any other woman. Since her mother was also a member, and Dorothy often brought great-grandchildren with her to the club, six generations of the Vohs family have attended.

My sister Miriam, a member until her recent death, was probably not at the first meeting, as school would have been in session, but she clearly remembered all the excitement when the club was being organized and the hours our mother spent on the phone getting it started.

When school was not in session, each member brought all her young children with her to the club. The kids had a party of their own, playing outside with one another and being served refreshments out the back door by the hostess.

That is where my memories of the club begin. I loved going and playing outside with all the neighbor kids. However, I *didn't* love the house cleaning frenzy my mother got into when *she* was the hostess. The club was so large that in order to seat everyone, we brought in planks of wood from the barn, rested each end of the board on nail kegs, and covered the boards with blankets to avoid splinters. We had to clean every corner of the house. My mother planned the refreshments for days in advance.

In my own adulthood, I became a member of the club when I had three small children. At that time, my mother was still alive and able to enjoy having a daughter who was also a member. We celebrated the club's 50th anniversary together. My own little family moved soon, and my mother's health made it hard for her to attend regularly after that celebration.

Now, thirty years later, I am again in the community and a member of the club. I celebrate and honor the vision of my mother and her friends for giving our community this club which has served our neighborhood well for so long.

Thanks, Mama.

Snakes in My Space

One thing that has not changed since I was a child is my aversion to snakes. I won't say I am afraid of snakes, but I sure don't like them. Since our home is set among many trees and very near a beautiful pond, we do see the creatures from time to time. That I can tolerate. What I don't like is to have them invading *my space*.

Last Sunday in Sunday School one of our class members told about finding a snake on her doorstep. She detailed the actions she took, which included an amputation on the snake. As we reached home, I thought about how brave she was to confront the intruder.

One of the first things I like to do on a sunny day when I arrive home is to open the inside door of our living room to let the sunlight in through the storm door. Since Sunday was a beautiful day, I headed for the door immediately. I was feeling grateful for our setting that allowed us to look out at the sparkling water and blue skies when I felt something unusual on the doorknob.

You guessed it! A small patterned snake was coiled tightly around the doorknob. Since it didn't move I, at first, thought our great-granddaughter had tied a cord around the knob. But closer inspection revealed it to be a small snake.

Thankfully, Lester was entering the house behind me. Forgetting women's lib and equality, I asked for his help. He couldn't believe his eyes. How did it reach the doorknob? Regardless of how it entered the house, this wasn't the time for debating. It was time for action.

Taking a cooking fork and a sack, Lester tried to pry the little fellow out of its circle and drop it into the bag for further inspection. He got it uncoiled, but instead of getting it into the bag, it fell to the floor where it quickly looked for a hiding place. Quick action and an open door got the snake kicked out onto the deck where it immediately disappeared through a crack in the floor.

I now know it is likely that more than one snake has resided under our deck, but knowing for sure that this particular guy is under there is not comforting. When I go outside to enjoy the moon, I will be very aware that I may have company. As long as it stays below me, I can relax. But if it tries to come calling again, I'll willingly follow my Sunday School friend's example and do some surgery.

I don't want to spend my middle age-plus years with a snake. I wouldn't mourn if the snake didn't reach old age, but if it does, I hope it will spend its golden years on the other side of the pond and not share our home.

What's Bugging Us

I know it is reported in Genesis that when God created the earth, He saw that it was good. But do you really suppose that God looked really hard at the chigger? I can see the benefit to the earth of snakes, even though I don't want them around me. I can see that the work of spiders, ants, and bees results in good for all species. But I have yet to see a use of chiggers unless it is to test our will power. Perhaps God enjoys seeing how long we can refrain from scratching a personal spot that a chigger has visited with its itching juice.

When I was a child and spent hours in the fields, on the grass, and walking in weeds, I got chiggers so badly that I even had bites in my hair. I scratched until they built up a nice little mound of hardened secretions. Now that I wash my hair much more often, I don't have that particular relationship with the little red bug. But the ones I have are usually quite personal and uncomfortable.

I have been told that our chiggers are what some Southerners call *jiggers*. I have not been able to research this insect enough to know for sure. I do know there are no chiggers in the East, or in the West. Texas has red ants but not chiggers. So if those parts of our nation can exist without this insect, I don't see why those of us in the Midwest are so blessed!

Visitors from other parts of the country sit down on our lawns without a care, not realizing what they are inviting. We had one relative call back to report that he had broken out in a rash every place that he had elastic or tight-fitting clothes. He was afraid he had been bitten by a tick. We reassured him that his trip into waist high weeds had caused this problem and not a tick bite.

In my childhood and youth, we didn't have ticks in Vernon County. I never saw a tick here until the late 1960s. Re-establishing deer in this area brought in the friendly little tick. Though ticks are not favorites of mine either, I feel much better about them than I do about the chigger. At least I can see them and can feel them crawling up on me before they stop for lunch.

I have nearly pulled a freckle off a grandchild, at times, thinking I spotted an embedded yearling tick. Since scientists inform us that insects will be around this old earth longer than humans, I guess we should get well acquainted with their benefits and habits and learn to appreciate them.

Personally, I am as well acquainted with a bunch of chiggers as I ever want to be. I won't let a microscopic red bug keep me from enjoying the summer, but I could enjoy it more without them.

The Thrashers Are Coming!

Yesterday I watched a neighbor combine a large field of wheat in one afternoon. He had the help of one person driving a truck to take the grain away, but otherwise he did the whole field by himself in about five hours.

It started me thinking about the long hours that our family and neighbors spent harvesting wheat in the good old days. First, the ripened grain was cut with a binder and bundles of wheat were left in the field with the grain heads still intact. If bad weather threatened, there would be a rush to collect the bundles and put them in a shock. The shock was then covered with a couple of the bundles to keep the rain from saturating the wheat as it stood in the field. These fields sometimes stayed this way for several days or weeks awaiting the next process, which was threshing.

In my memory, when the threshing machine came into the neighborhood, the local farmers all came to work as a crew to repay their neighbors for helping them. Occasionally, someone worked for wages, but usually, except for the threshing machine operators, neighbors traded work.

Several farmers brought their horses and wagons. Their job was to go around the field and fork the bundles from the shocks onto the wagon. The wagon then moved to the threshing machine. The farmer who owned the land selected the spot for the machine to allow the best place for the straw stack.

As the bundles were forked onto the moving belts of the threshing machine, the grain came out a spout into a waiting grain wagon. The straw was blown into a large stack for later use as animal food, bedding, shelter, or to fill a wet spot in the field.

The grain wagon then took the grain to the farmer's granary, to a commercial elevator, or in some cases directly to Ellis to the *Katy* railroad where a freight car waited on a siding.

When all the fields in one farm were finished, sometimes taking several days or a week, the machines and men moved the whole process onto the next farm. This was quite a difference from our modern day neighbor with his one helper completing the job in hours.

But I have left out the best part—feeding the threshers. The women dreaded this ordeal. Cooking enough food to feed a dozen or so hungry men on a hot July day was bad enough. But the odor of that many hard-working men gathered in one hot dining room or kitchen before the days of air conditioners was an experience in itself.

Some of the men filled their plates and took a cold glass of iced tea outside to drink while eating in the fresh air. There they could take a little rest while parked under a big shade tree.

The women, as their husbands did, helped one another out and often were on the serving and cooking line for several days in each other's homes. I have not talked to any middle age-plus women who express regret at not having to prepare and serve these harvest meals each summer.

In fact, I think some still have nightmares when they hear the words "Hey, Mom, the thrashers are coming!"

Old-Time Snacks

I like to have a snack nearby when I am relaxing with a book or a television program. Yesterday, I discovered we were out of chips, the cookies were gone, and the microwave popcorn was used up. As I was searching for something, anything, to eat, I began remembering the treats we enjoyed as children.

A treat was to take the paraffin off the top of the jelly jars and chew it like gum. As long as the jelly flavor remained, it was a delicious treat. When the flavor did disappear, we could always add another bit of jelly to our wad of paraffin or turn to the sugar bowl to freshen up the chaw. Sometimes, we even saved the paraffin from day to day in case there was not another jar of jelly to scalp for a new treat.

We loved to take half a piece of bread, roll it into a cone shape, and put a dab of jelly at the top. It was like eating a jelly-bread cone. This was especially good if the bread was homemade and still warm.

Our lawn had several apple trees in the corner. I recall that one particular Jonathan apple tree bore plentiful amounts of fruit each year. Since we couldn't wait until the apples became ripe to enjoy them, we climbed up into the tree and ate the green apples while we were safely out of sight of adults or older siblings. I don't remember ever having a stomach ache after these experiences, but now just eating a few slices of a ripe apple can cause some discomfort. Maybe it is a delayed reaction.

On hot days, we used the icepick to chip off a small piece of ice from the block in the icebox. We'd sprinkle it generously with salt and suck on it as it melted down our clothes, adding to the cooling effect.

When I was visiting the Kafers, armed with a salt shaker, I loved to go with Joyce to her grandfather's garden and eat a ripe tomato right off the vine. This couldn't happen too often because he was very protective of his beautiful garden.

These memories have made me very hungry, and although my middle age-plus tastes have changed, the fun of our homemade treats reminds me that snacks don't have to come packaged in paper and boxes.

And for those of you who are worried about all that sugar, I can report that my teeth are still my own and are fairly sound—not pretty, but sound.

Cats Who Have Owned Me

Cats are my favorite pets. In fact, I don't think I've been without a cat for more than a year or two in my whole life. Even when I was in college, our landlady's cat had kittens in our closet. We ended up adopting two of them as our own.

Two cats stand out as special. My sister and I purchased one in eastern Vernon County when I was a teenager. Sir Cuthbert the Gleep was a red Persian we bought for one dollar from Mrs. Ozzenberger over near Dederick. This cat made several car trips back and forth from Washington D.C. to Nevada. He walked on a leash. We had a cat carrier that we took into hotels with his litter box and cat food inside, but Cuthbert would grandly walk into the lobby on a leash. He would hold his glorious tail erect, swishing it back and forth. I enjoyed the attention our procession brought. My mother merely endured the process.

Cats were not her favorite animal, but she did get quite fond of Cuthbert.

The other special cat was Maxi, named for his long fur coat that came to his feet, as the style for women's dresses was then. Since his litter mate Mini died quite young, Maxi was the lord of the household for fifteen years. He was born in the basement of our parsonage in Butler and died under our bed in our parsonage in Versailles. In between, he lived in two other parsonages and was always a well-behaved and affectionate cat. Although he was supposed to be our son Mark's cat, he lived long after Mark left home.

At present, we have Wynken, Blynken and Nod, who are basically outdoor cats (until they meow at the door, and then they come inside with me).

Middle age-plus folk seem to have two differing ideas about pets. Some don't want to be bothered. They want to be free to travel and be away for long periods of time without the responsibility of a pet. Others make the pets their second family; they call each other Mama and Daddy to the pets and spend lots of money on the animals.

I don't believe in reincarnation, but, just in case, I place my order for my next life to be a cat owned by someone like me. I want someone who is easily trainable to do my bidding, willing to let me live my own life, but happy to include me in the family life when I wish. Also, I'd like my own pet door. Of course, I prefer to eat human food, straight from the family table, and want a comfortable bed to share with a family member *if* I wish. I hope, if this should come to pass, that there are other suckers out there I could train to give me the care I desire. I'd hate to risk trying to train a dog lover!

Pomp and Circumstance

Nothing brings a lump to my throat quicker than hearing a school band play "Pomp and Circumstance" while watching a new group of students marching down the aisle to their graduation ceremony.

Visions of my own graduations and those of my children and grandchildren add to the emotion of seeing yet another group of youngsters finish their public schooling.

High school graduations seem more important today than graduations from college or other advanced training courses. High school graduation often means the end of living at home, the end of running with the old crowd, and the end of other people setting your schedule and standards.

The middle age-plus generation usually experienced other graduations that were important before they reached the big high school graduation.

It was common for rural schools to have an eighth grade graduation ceremony. In order for students to participate in this ceremony and to officially finish the grade school curriculum, they gathered several school districts in the area to take a standardized test under the direction of the County Superintendent of Schools.

My older brothers and sisters, who attended one-room Pleasant Ridge School, took this test in Deerfield, a village four miles away. My brother Harold was so excited and scared to be at this bigger school in the big town that he couldn't concentrate on the test. He failed. He had to take the eighth grade over. He went on to graduate from George Washington University in Washington, D.C., and has had a successful career in which he continues to serve as a consultant at the age of ninety-one. He has lived in New York City and Chicago as well as our nation's capital, but none of these cities affected him like the busyness of Deerfield. It scared this thirteen-year-old country boy.

All of my public school education was in Washington. Our graduations were from the sixth grade and then from the ninth grade in junior high before the bigger high school graduation.

What I remember most about my junior high graduation was that the student body sang an anthem as part of the ceremony. The music teacher asked about twenty of us from this class of three hundred to mouth the words of the anthem for fear that our off-tune voices would mar the performance. For years, I wouldn't sing in public, even in a group. My high school prom was in a downtown D.C. hotel.

Because of wartime regulations against using cars for social reasons, we had to ride to the prom on the city bus or the streetcar.

When we were one block from our destination, we had to leave the streetcar for a shelter during an air-raid drill. We ended up walking the last block to the prom after the all-clear sounded. My date stepped on the hem of my formal dress, my hair drooped because of the walk in the night air, and my high heels were killing me. But we did attend our prom.

Many schools try to have their graduations in the football stadium to allow more seating and to avoid the heat of a gymnasium in late May. Often the weather does not cooperate, necessitating last minute changes to move everything hastily into the gym. However, most of the details get lost in memory while the emotion of the day remains fixed in our minds.

Goodbye youth; hello adulthood. Down the road in not too many years these young people will be joining us as middle age-plus. Best wishes to each on this journey.

G.I. Bill Memories

The school bell is ringing again these mornings. It doesn't seem possible that it is that time again. But what seems even less possible is that our older grandchildren are going back to school, not to grade school, or even to high school, but to college!

These little tykes that just last year were burping on our shoulders are now living the college life. I hope they are *not* burping on anyone's shoulder these days.

When we go on campus to visit, the familiar buildings we knew are still there, but sometimes they are hard to find among all the new structures. Beautiful campus areas are changed into parking lots, dormitories are everywhere, and apartments for married students are as plentiful as the dorms for single students used to be.

The middle age-plus generation often went to college either right before, during, or after World War II. (I used to say after the war, but my kids asked if it was the Civil War!)

In those days, cars were a rarity on campus. Those who did have cars didn't have gas for them because of rationing; all dating and other social activities were done on foot.

When the service men returned on the G.I. bill, the campus changed radically. The enrollment jumped to twice the wartime rate. There was not enough housing, and women were trying to get their PHT degree (Putting Hubby Through). Many brides had finished college during the war, and when their guys returned, the priority was for the men to get their degrees.

Lester and I were lucky. As an agriculture student, he knew about an old farm house that was part of a pending estate hearing. For safety, the owners wanted someone to live in the house. We got the use of a nine-room house full of antique furniture. Some small flaws existed. There was no heat until we resurrected an old cook stove and a coal-burning room heater. Water was from a pump in the backyard, and the outhouse was about to fall down.

We were privileged, since many of our friends were living in converted bars, garage apartments that still had car grease on the floors, or one-room apartments with a bath shared with four other families. In fact, we were so privileged we shared the upstairs with another couple.

Recently, we visited our grandson and his family in a sparkling new two-bedroom university apartment, complete with large bath, equipped kitchen, air conditioning, and telephone with call waiting. I thought back to our university housing. We had lots of air conditioning, especially in the winter. The kitchen was equipped with a two-burner kerosene stove and an icebox on the back porch. But we always had the advantage of looking forward to better days. You see, each little luxury we gained was a milestone we celebrated. We had nowhere to go but up.

I'm glad our loved ones are comfortable. But I wish for them the excitement we experienced when we covered over the cracks in the outhouse walls so that the winds didn't freeze our bottoms so badly. I hope they can share such happiness.

I Am Somebody

Those of us who are middle age-plus are often faced with the realization that younger people among us have no idea what we have accomplished in our lifetimes. Often we are lumped together as little old ladies (or men) in tennis shoes or the blue hair bunch.

Even though I am now in this category (not the *little* old lady or the blue hair), I often find myself falling into this trap. When I meet someone for the first time who is in my age group, I sometimes neglect learning about that person.

We forget that all of us started as children and have gone through various life stages before reaching our present age. The facts that we were great on roller skates, could ride a horse bareback, directed a huge corporation, or organized all the church dinners for ten years doesn't occur to a new acquaintance. We lose much interesting information and understanding when this happens.

I must admit that part of this is our fault. Since we resist being categorized as merely part of the older group, we bore others with stories about our earlier life, forgetting who has heard them and repeat too often. But the stories are worth hearing.

As a child, it was almost impossible for me to realize that my parents were once children. I looked at the old pictures without seeing anything of the persons my parents were at that time. Even baby pictures of my older siblings were hard for me to understand. My own baby pictures were also a puzzle as I saw everything in the present.

Now I find myself having some of the same problems when I meet new friends in my age group. I know they were children about the time I was, but when I hear some of their experiences, I find it hard to picture this sedate, dignified man putting a cow on the barn roof at Halloween or the sweet-faced lady hiding behind the barn to smoke.

The new city directory lists the occupations of adults in the family. But if the adults are retired, the occupation space simply says, "Retired." I think it would be nice to put retired teacher or retired farmer, so we will know more about one another.

Since our society tends to value people for what they do for a living, my generation feels somewhat devalued when we are listed as retired. It does imply that we once did *something,* but no one really cares what it was we did. Maybe that is why I found it tempting to come out of retirement so I could put an occupation after my name again. I guess I don't want to be listed as just Carolyn Gray Thornton, *Has Been.*

Metropolitan Small Town Helpfulness

My week has been a jumble of unexpected happenings and changed plans. The few times I get my life organized to have most days planned out in detail, things have a way of changing all my plans.

I had no outside commitments during this week, so I planned to use the days for some fine tuning on our lawn, to do a bit of spring cleaning (I try to get it done each year before winter), to plan a series of meetings we were to host during the first weeks of the month, and to just enjoy the freedom from commitments.

I did get parts of the lawn mowed in between the rainy days, and I bought a few supplies for the gatherings to be held in our home as well as doing two loads of laundry. Period.

The rest of my plans vanished in a flurry of doctor and hospital visits as my husband's right eye began to show signs of something seriously wrong. It came to a climax with an 8:30 p.m. surgery in Menorah Hospital in Kansas City. My husband had a torn retina.

Even though we once lived in metropolitan Kansas City for three years, I did not enjoy the traffic problems and speed of the cars while I was trying to locate a place new to me. Either the traffic moves faster now than fifteen years ago, or I may be a little older, but when I am driving on the inside lane of eight different lanes of traffic and discover that I need to be in the outside lane within a half mile to make my turn, I begin yearning for the traffic on Austin Street in Nevada.

Our experiences with the personnel at each of the offices and at the hospital were very pleasant. With one exception, each person we met was very kind, attentive, and helpful. I began to realize that one advantage of being middle age-plus is that others sometimes do go out of their way to be helpful. For example, since Menorah Hospital is a Jewish facility, and my husband chose Yom Kipper to have his emergency, the hospital was not fully staffed. When I was wandering the halls looking for a specific area, someone always offered directions or even walked a portion of the way with me to be sure I reached my designation.

The fine specialist that did the surgery at the end of his religious holiday spent a long time with me afterwards explaining the whole procedure and stressing the need for Lester to do very little for several days.

All our plans for hosting several events in our home had to be changed, and the reason for deep housecleaning could be delayed for another season or two.

As a final emphasis for our week of experiences, when we were ready to leave the hospital the next morning, I went to get the car while the nurse wheeled Lester to the front door. I relaxed into the familiar car seat ready to begin the trip home. The car wouldn't start.

Thankfully, the man at the information desk suggested we call security. A uniformed officer jump-started the car for me, and we were on our way home. After several minutes on the road, we noticed that the dome light was on, and I remembered that our great-granddaughter had asked me about those lights in the ceiling of the car while we were waiting for the school bus. So the problem was caused at home and only showed up while in the city. The people in the city were just as helpful as the ones here in Vernon County would have been if the problem had surfaced nearby.

In spite of TLC treatment everywhere we went, it was great to get back home with a relatively intact husband, a car that would start, and familiar scenes on every side of our one-lane graveled road.

Vacation War Department Job

Memory is a fickle friend sometimes. I have been told that I have a very good memory (except for names), but there are some things that have completely left my memory bank. I can perfectly recall incidents that happened during a certain time period but completely forget something else during that same time.

One of the things I dislike about being middle age-plus is that I tend to wake up too early in the morning. Since I don't want to disturb my husband or others who might be sleeping at our home, I quietly stay in bed until a more civilized time to get up. However, my mind does not remain quiet but travels through all sorts of mental twists down memory lane or ahead to the day's activities.

This morning as I lay in the darkness, I began thinking about the Christmas holidays of 1942. We lived in Washington, D.C., where I was a senior at Woodrow Wilson High School. A request came to the school to have thirty students work at one of the temporary war department buildings during the Christmas holidays. The hours were from 7:00 a.m. to 3:00 p.m. at a building clear across town. These students had to rank in the upper half of the class, have parental permission, and be recommended by a teacher. My friend Betty Bettles and I decided this would be fun; we could always use the money.

The teacher I asked for a recommendation tried to talk me out of it by saying that I didn't need the money and should just enjoy the vacation, but she gave me a recommendation anyway. My father said he couldn't see me getting up, ready to leave the house at 6:00 a.m. for ten days, but he signed the form.

With this negative support from a favorite teacher and my father, I was determined to make a good record on this job. Here is where my memory lapses come in to play. Betty lived near Wisconsin Avenue where we were to take the streetcar to start our long commute across town. I lived almost a mile away from her. Since it was wartime, we couldn't use cars, and I have no memory of how I got from our home on Nevada Avenue to Wisconsin Avenue before 6:00 a.m. It would have been dark, and the brownouts of wartime made the streets very dim. I suppose I walked the mile, but I have no memory of that. I do clearly remember the reaction of the regular riders when our bunch of high school girls and boys boarded the streetcar and nearly filled the seats. There were almost audible groans from those seasoned workers who wanted to nap or read on their way to work.

Our responsibility was to check the work of the crew who worked the night shift. Though we were sworn to secrecy about the work, none of us really understood what it was all about. We had a model sheet to go by while checking what the night crew had written on their sheets. In this day of copy machines, computers, and fax machines, it is almost like the dark ages to realize that these sheets of detailed instructions had to be copied onto other sheets in order to send them to all the places that needed them. Our job was to see that they were copied correctly.

As we all worked in the same area and had the same lunch break, it didn't seem too foreign to us until we went into the employees' cafeteria. While we were mingled with all the other workers, we had one of our first opportunities to be in an equal working relationship with people of other races and cultures. It is hard to believe today that we could have reached the age of seventeen or eighteen without having experienced a bi-racial environment.

We evidently did a good job of proofreading because we finished the backlog and ran out of work to do before the ten-day vacation was over. The last day we worked, I left early because my father called to see if I could meet the family at Occidental Restaurant on F Street. I got permission, left my sack lunch with a co-worker, and joined the family downtown.

Although I can't remember how I got to the streetcar, I do recall that my father ordered pig knuckles and sauerkraut to eat. And I remember that I bought a combination record player/radio with part of the forty dollars I earned at this first job. I kept this radio-record player through college but can't remember what ultimately happened to it. It may be somewhere in all our stuff. I can't remember.

7

Tis' The Season Of Unexpected Beauty

In old age they still produce fruit; they are always green and full of sap.

Psalm 92:14

Nature's First Green

My crocus bulbs are blooming! What a glorious feeling it is to look outside after this dreary winter and see these brave little purple, yellow, and white flowers decorating the lawn. After all the cloudy and rainy days, I was not expecting to see these spots of beauty when they suddenly appeared. Their arrival brought me outside to survey other areas of the lawn where I found daffodils and tulip leaves beginning to peek out, buds on the forsythia bushes beginning to swell, and cardinals singing their mating calls.

The awareness that winter is almost over makes all things more exiting and beautiful. Nothing is quite as ugly in Missouri as the last part of winter when the snows are usually gone, the greening has not begun, and everything is a dull brown. But this drabness makes the coming of spring more spectacular. I wouldn't want to live where I couldn't feel the joy of green-up time.

Our lives experience this same cycle at times. We go through dull, dreary days that seem to have no end, and then something delightful bursts into our lives like my little crocus flowers. It might be a call from a long time friend, an unexpected compliment or honor, a letter from a family member, or the discovery of a very good book. Some little brightness can change the gloom of our days as quickly as the first sight of these harbingers of spring.

My week has been filled with promises that happy events can bring. A family wedding (grandson) brought together many friends and relatives as we celebrated this new start for a couple. A stalled car brought a new friend who found the problem and corrected it for me. A Sunday School class accepted my role as teacher by 100% attendance. A phone call came from a brother saying he may visit soon. And an outfit I had ordered arrived and fit nicely.

These events were made brighter and happier because of the mood these little flowers awoke within me. Then I knew that nice things have always been happening to me, but I had missed some of the joy because of my winter-related gloom.

Now spring is arriving. I will meet the world head on with excitement, commitment, and gladness. I will walk that mile each day that is good for my health. And while I am walking, I will watch for each new sign of spring along the way. I will eat my seven fruits and vegetables each day, and I will rise early to get all my work done quickly.

Yes, I will do all these things when spring arrives. But on the calendar there are eight more days of winter. Maybe I'll just sleep in a few more times or watch an old movie on television. I will have plenty of time for these other things when spring officially arrives. After all, each season does have some benefits!

A Goosey Blessed Event

For the last month we have eagerly awaited a blessed event at our farm. For the past few years a pair of Canada geese has chosen our pond as its nesting place. We marked the date when the female began sitting on her eggs and knew that this was the week for the eggs to hatch.

As the week progressed, we could tell something was about to happen by the actions of the mother and the big gander who had been patiently patrolling the pond and nest site. Finally, on Friday we noticed activity in the nest. Our pond is low, and since early spring when we put new bedding in the nest, the pole had shifted in such a way that the cutout side of this wildlife conservation nest was tilted up instead of level. Therefore, when the eggs hatched, the little ones seemed to have trouble getting out of the nest.

Toward the end of the day, one adventuresome gosling plopped down to the water where the gander immediately came to protect and guide the little one. But after that, for hours, nothing happened in spite of numerous trips the mother took off the nest and calls and commands from both parents.

We watched through our binoculars and saw there were at least two more in the nest, but they weren't trying very hard to leave. (Those of us middle age-plus have had similar experience with our offspring wanting to stay in the nest!)

Darkness stopped us from keeping tabs on the family, but at dawn's early light we saw the gander with one little fuzzy shadow following him, and the goose in the nest with some other balls of fuzz.

Since we knew that the ingredients in the egg were designed to supply the young with food for only the first twenty-four hours, we worried that the nestlings would starve, or at least weaken so they wouldn't ever be able to get out. We tried to go near the nest with a hoe in an attempt to pull the nest lower down but were met with attacks from both parents.

A second gosling suddenly took the plunge and joined his father and sibling in the water. Since there were still some in the nest, Lester decided it was time to act. He made a cage of woven wire to protect his upper body from the adults and waded out to the nest. The gander started honking from across the pond but was slowed by his two little followers which he would not leave. The goose rose up, flapping her wings, and in fright and excitement, three more baby goslings jumped overboard. Although protesting loudly, the family swam to the other side of the pond.

A look into the nest verified that the family was complete, so Lester straightened the nest and watched the happy family that never realized that we were really its friends.

Listen to the Mockingbird

I have always loved mockingbirds. Their constant variety of songs cheers up each hot summer day, and watching the antics of the male birds is great fun.

There is at least one pair of mockingbirds that lives in or near our lawn. I usually see the male sitting on top of the highest rung of our television antenna. If he is not there, he is at the top of the power pole. He doesn't sit on the wires leading to the pole like the swallows do. No, he gets to the very highest spot on top of the pole itself.

I wonder if he prefers these lofty perches to see farther or to see better? For whatever reason, he sits there singing the songs of all the birds in the area for hours on end. From listening to him, you would think we have dozens of birds on our pole, but it is the one lone mockingbird singing his heart out.

After watching him sing several minutes, I notice that he leaves his perch, flies about four feet in the air, and then returns to sing again. I suppose he stops to get a drink or some feed, but almost any time we are outside, we can spot him on one of these two high places.

When the windows are open at night, especially when moonlight brightens the night sky, we can still hear him warbling away.

Many questions come to my mind as I listen to our friend. How does he decide which song to sing next? Does he have a preset pattern he follows by instinct, or does he sing just what comes into his mind at the moment? I can't discern any repeated pattern in the variety. Sometimes he imitates the cardinal for several minutes without a break. Other times, he seems to alternate songs quickly from one bird to another. I assume that this singing is meant to attract the female bird, but I don't see him with another bird or even helping with nesting duties. Maybe his role is to teach the young all the different songs. I'm sure there are books that could answer my questions, but it is more fun to sit outside listening to his repertoire and wondering about his life.

This brings up questions also about the functions of some of our practices and antics. Lula Welborn told me that her young grandson sings at the top of his lungs when he is mowing her lawn on the riding mower. As I laughed at her story, I remembered that I also sing when I am mowing. The sound of the mower drowns out my voice, even to myself, but I have the joy of singing loudly without fear of others hearing who would criticize. (And if they actually heard, they would criticize!) I don't know if Lula's grandson sings for the same reason, but we all know many who sing in the shower where they can hear their voices and feel powerful as they sing.

My nephew who lives in Colorado dreams of climbing every mountain in the state that is over 14,000 feet. Is his desire to reach the very tops of high mountains the same urge that causes our mockingbird to perch on the two highest objects in our lawn? Do we like to be on top and look out on a broad expanse of land so that we can feel we have conquered part of our surroundings? My father used to play the song "Listen to the Mockingbird" with a swing rhythm that I loved. Though the words to the song are not as cheery as the tune, I loved hearing the song. But my attraction to the bird occurred before I heard my father play the song; there was a period when I didn't even know my father could play the piano. When he bought a good Baldwin grand piano for my sister and me, he suddenly began playing again. This song was the first one I heard him play. The excitement of that moment is reflected each time I hear the song or hear the little show-off bird sing.

Now that I am middle age-plus and never learned to play with the feeling our father put into his music, I still enjoy music made by other humans or by the birds. I've decided that the most important word in that song title is *Listen.* There is much music to hear, with even more variety than our little mockingbird offers.

Maybe next time I'll write about the bullfrogs' music echoing from our pond.

Resurrection Symbol

Sometimes things that we have worked on carefully for days will not come to pass while other things fall into our laps without any effort on our part. An example of this happened to us recently.

I have worked diligently to get special plants to grow in and around our house. Some of them do okay, but others, despite our efforts, never make it. Many of the greenhouses say that if a plant doesn't grow, they will return your money. By the time I know the plant isn't going to grow, I have forgotten where I bought it, and if I did remember, I wouldn't have saved the proof that I did buy the plant at that particular greenhouse.

But without any effort on my part, I now have a beautiful gourd vine loaded with multi-colored gourds of various shapes and sizes. A couple of years ago when my late sister Miriam moved into her new apartment, our good friend Opal Hensley gave her a cute basket of gourds she had raised herself. After the death of my sister, I kept the basket which had pleased her so much. Sadly, after about a year, the gourds began to smell, so I reluctantly threw them onto the compost heap behind our house. I hated to do this because in the meantime our friend Opal had also died. The little basket was a bond between both of these women, and although I kept the basket, I couldn't save the gourds.

Then a month ago, we noticed a lush vine growing out of our compost pile. We first assumed it was a cantaloupe vine, but soon it was apparent we were wrong. Small colorful gourds appeared all over the vine, which had grown up the wire enclosure.

As if a resurrection symbol, the rotting gourds produced dozens of new ornamental gourds for our enjoyment. I watch these gifts daily for they have become a link between loved ones. I look forward to displaying them in our home when the time is right to pick them. I also hope to share, following the example of the generous grower.

Maybe it is a lesson to let us know that the whole world doesn't depend on our own efforts. Sometimes if we just sit back and relax, things will happen, even without our direct supervision.

After years of parenting, grandparenting, and now, great-grandparenting, and after having responsibilities in agencies, churches, and clubs, it is hard to think that things will continue without my help. Younger people will pick up the slack if I relax a little. And maybe everything didn't really have to be done just as I did it. There can always be a better way or a different person to do what is needed.

As we reach middle age-plus, it can be hard to recognize that we aren't absolutely essential to the well-being of the world. We also don't want to believe that what we worked so hard for didn't matter.

I believe that the work of each of us is important, but sometimes we won't understand it until later. So it is with the labor of love that our friend gave us--the original gift of beauty--and now, unexpectedly, she's given us even more enjoyment. Our labors keep on producing for years, and sometimes the best things happen even without our help.

Who would have thought that I could learn so much from a gourd?

Unexpected Beauty

Isn't it funny how things that first seem to be a problem turn out to be a blessing? The other day the road grader on our crushed rock road left a pile of dirt and gravel in a ridge at the side of the road. This created a barrier too big for the tractor-pulled mowers to cut without denting the mower blades on the rocks. Therefore, the nicely-mowed shoulders by the fields stopped suddenly right at the edge of the road, leaving a foot-wide row of weeds.

Each time we passed, I mentally cut off the offending weeds so that in my mind it all looked as neat as the rest of the right-of-way. In reality, however, the weeds grew taller and stronger.

Then, as if overnight, suddenly those weeds burst forth with brilliant yellow Spanish blossoms and black-eyed Susans. Now when we pass on the road, we are cheered along the way with a border of gold. Across the fence, there are patches of the same glorious flowers in areas where the hay mowers missed or couldn't reach and where no cattle have grazed.

One of the favorite memories of my teenage years is riding Princess Peggy (a horse my sister and I had for a few years) across an unplowed field that was thick with these same yellow blossoms.

At that time, our whole farm was planted in wheat, but my father let some fields lie fallow to improve the fertility. In late summer or early fall, these fields became as colorful as a Disney movie scene. Ellen and I relished sunset horseback rides through this paradise.

When I saw the recent road border of flowers, I was transported back to that feeling of exhilaration from almost sixty years ago.

I love the colors that nature gives us for the beginning and ending of the growing season. Yellow and gold greet us in the spring, with our forsythia bushes and the yellow of the willow branches. In the fall, the season's farewell is colored with goldenrod and my favorite Spanish blossom and black-eye Susans.

I hope no one will mow until these flowers have faded. My memories need this wake-up call each day as I go to town.

The next time I fuss at the road grader for the method of preparing our road, I will remember the unexpected gift given our neighborhood with the rocky ledge by the side of the road.

I'll Miss My Friend

I lost a good friend this week. My friend did not die but was killed because it would soon be dead. The elm tree that shaded our front patio was dying of Dutch elm disease and was becoming a danger and a nuisance with dropping limbs, leaves, and bark. But I hated to see it go!

This tree had sprouted on its own near the old trailer we had put on our farm years ago to have a get-away while my husband was still in the active ministry. We set our picnic table under its small branches when it was young, and as it aged and grew, so did our homestead. The old trailer was replaced with a modular home which we've added onto gradually until now there is a nice deck off of an indoor-outdoor living room near the place of the elm tree. We depended on its limbs to shade our outside activities although we knew that it would probably soon die as elm trees do in this Dutch elm disease-ridden area.

We realized this summer would be its last as the leaves began to wither on the top, and the bark pulled away from its trunkful of blemishes. Leaves continually dropped. The tree would soon die.

This week we decided it was time to take the tree down before it infected any of the other elms and before the branches fell on us or the house. We cut it down and sawed the wood into convenient lengths for our wood-burning stove. We hauled the branches off to a ditch to stop erosion.

As I have watched the rise and decline of my friend, the tree, I've been struck with the similarities between its life and those of middle age-plus. First, we are young and spontaneous, growing into new uses. Then we reach a mature stage where we are relied on for many things. Later, signs of aging dot the top of our heads and, like the bark, our skin shows blemishes and hangs loosely. We urgently need to be useful, and we hope to give warmth and comfort to others as a last gift.

This morning as I looked out the window while the sun was rising, I noticed the big gap in the foliage where my friend had stood. But I also noticed young oak trees growing near the elm were in better view. I could see the shape of their slender trunks and branches and realized that the older elm had kept some of those branches from the perfect shape they were intended to take. I could see the clouds more clearly with the elm gone and noticed more birds flying in the sky.

I will miss my friend but will enjoy watching these young oaks grow straight and strong. I will enjoy the warmth of a winter fire as my friend continues to serve us.

Fall Back

Here we go again. Spring forward, fall back. Daylight saving time will end. We will drive to work in daylight and drive home as it gets dark. That adjustment isn't too bad, but setting my internal alarm is a little trickier. I will continue to wake and get sleepy at my regular times, but gradually I will adjust to that, also. Resetting my clocks is one of the biggest pains—especially the one in my car. The whole process seems needless to me. Daylight saving time is like making a blanket longer by cutting a foot off the top and sewing it to the bottom.

I remember when daylight saving time was adopted nationwide. There was a lot of talk about the pros and cons of the idea. One woman told me in all seriousness that she thought that would be too much sun for her tomato plants. Others worried about their livestock schedules. There are still times when someone arrives an hour early or an hour late because of the time change, but most of us take it in stride and go on about our business with little disruption.

Back in the 1960s, when daylight saving was a decision made locally, by city or by county, we lived in Archie, Missouri. We could leave Archie after church was over and arrive in Nevada at my parent's home for Sunday dinner at twelve noon! Setting meetings was very confusing because some of the people attending were on "God's time" and some were on "government time."

Many of us remember when we were on year-round "war time" during World War II. I was in high school in Washington, D.C. Since the capital was in a continual brownout because of the war, going to school in the morning during the winter could be a gloomy procedure. Since we weren't allowed to use our cars for nonessential trips, I walked the mile from our home to the school on streets without lights. The school was a very welcome sight in the dim early morning hours.

That experience has made me appreciate sunlight and moonlight. These bright October days with the sun shining on colorful leaves lifts my spirits. The memories of those brownout days disappear quickly as the sun warms my body, and the moonlight caresses me. I look forward to each new moon and watch for the increasing brightness of nights.

This Sunday when we wake, we can enjoy the brighter morning and try to forget that it will be dark an hour earlier in the evening. Each bit of light can cheer us no matter what the hour or what heavenly body sends the light to us.

The Sense of a Goose

A nice thing about all the cold icy weather we had early in January is that it makes us really appreciate the ordinary winter days, with temperatures in the forties or fifties, and night time just at the freezing mark. Compared to New York, Chicago, and other northern places, we really had it good, even in our worst weather.

But today as I am writing, it is rather sunny, the temperature is quite comfortable, and because of this, our geese have returned. And they have returned with many of their buddies, distant relatives, and strangers. The field north of the house, which has nothing planted in it at this time, but had been plowed after the soybeans were harvested, was the site of a goose gathering yesterday. There were both Canada geese and snow geese mingling together. The snow geese, at times, would take to the air and circle around for a few minutes and then come back to graze again on the field.

The two types of geese, with markedly different coloring, were grazing together peacefully. When we returned from church and an early afternoon meeting, we noticed that they had visited our iced-over pond. Though becoming rotten, the ice still covers the whole pond. But yesterday afternoon several channels in the ice had been broken.

Other times we have witnessed the geese finding their way to the water when the pond was slightly frozen. They land on the ice (and that is comical to watch since they slide several feet on the ice, just as we clumsy humans would) and then they hunker down on one spot until their body heat melts the ice under them a bit. With their feet, they break the ice under their bodies. Instead of just staying in that one cleared spot, they move a little farther away and do the same thing. Eventually, they are able to combine the two or three cleared spots into an area where they can actually swim a bit. When several dozen geese do this at once, they can open a fairly large portion of the pond.

Since yesterday's channels were not long, we guessed that the ice was still too thick for them to be very successful. However, because of the rain and melting ground out in the field, they had plenty of water to drink, if not to swim in.

When it was too dark last night to see, I still heard the feathered friends visiting with each other. At dawn this morning, they were gone. Now they are beginning to circle in the sky again, so maybe we will have another group visit today.

People have warned us with dire threats that we will be sorry if the geese get too plentiful; they will become a problem for us. We have one family of geese that takes up residence with us each spring until their eggs hatch and then they leave with their little ones. This parent couple will not tolerate any other geese staying on the pond while they are forming their yearly family. They will drive away any other pair of geese and especially any lone goose. They tolerate ducks that occasionally come by but no geese. Possibly for this reason we have never had any over population on our pond or lawn. The ones who graze in the field probably have their head-quarters elsewhere and just visit us for an outing.

As far as we can tell, the only effects of our goosey friends are some free fertilizer in the fields, some weeds eaten at the edge of the pond, and a lot of amusement and education for our family who love to watch them.

We wish they would let us know where they go when they leave and introduce us to their grown children the next year when they return. We would like to know what they think of us as the ever-watchful gander sees every movement we make. And we are curious about different body movements and sounds they make when meeting other geese.

There is one thing we are really sure of after watching our friends for several years. We can really learn a lot from a goose.

What Was I Thinking?

Something is going around, and I have caught it. It happens to me each January. There is a wonderful break in the weather, and the sun shines in the windows. Then it happens. Seed catalogs start arriving. We have received four already.

I have told you that I am not much of a gardener, but I do love trees, shrubs, and flowers. I love to see them—not plant them. But when I look at these catalogs while sitting indoors on a sunny January day, I am suddenly empowered with *green thumbitis*. I see myself merrily planting this row of hedge bushes, preparing a bed of flowers for the hummingbirds and butterflies to enjoy, and spading up an area in our lawn for wild flowers.

The prices seem fairly reasonable; the illustrations are magnificent. I can picture us sitting out on the deck enjoying luscious blooms all summer.

I usually weaken and place an order or two. Then a terrible thing happens. This stuff actually arrives! It usually comes when I already have six things going at once or else the weather is terrible. And one thing is sure. I will have lost my enthusiasm.

Those dead-looking sprigs wrapped in mailing paper don't inspire me as the full color illustrations in the catalogs did. I even find it hard to remember what I actually did order. The twigs and bulbs in the packages don't look at all like I expected, and the names don't ring a bell.

A person who is better organized could go back to a copy of the order, refer to the picture in the catalog, and carry out the January dream, but that would be a person who is better at organization. The catalogs have gone to recycling. If I had a duplicate of the order slip, I have no idea where I put it for safekeeping, and my check stub merely gives the amount I spent back on that misplaced day in January.

We do have some trees and flowering shrubs that do their thing year after year without my help. I will probably get a few small plants to put in pots on the deck when the time comes, but these creations of my imagination in January have not fared well in the past. One of the great advantages about being middle age-plus is that the feeble efforts of several years do accumulate eventually to make a small showing of beauty in the lawn.

So if I catch this January bug, maybe one or two plants will actually live and grow, and maybe I will live long enough to see part of the imagined beauty the catalogs promised. January is half over, and I haven't weakened. I've always wanted a pussy willow bush. I'll try just once more.

8

Old Friends and New Neighbors

You have to grow old before somebody will tell you that you look young for your age.

Milton Berle

Topics of Conversation

Some people have asked it if isn't hard to think of something to talk about with your spouse when you have been married over fifty years. I have to laugh at their ignorance. There is much to talk about each day. Almost every morning there is a conversation about why the toaster doesn't toast the bread correctly after it has been adjusted or "Have you seen my purse?"

Other long talks can revolve around plans for meals. You get to discuss not only what you might eat, but, since schedules are varied in middle age-plus years, you can also discuss when you will eat.

Cars passing on the road create other opportunities. "Was that the mail that passed, or was that Bill in his truck?" If it was the mail, there are unlimited possibilities to talk about all the chances we receive to become millionaires. There is also the fun of deciding who will pay which bill.

As we separate to take care of our different responsibilities, there are many times when meaningful conversations occur. Sometimes when completely alone and I ask myself, "What did I come into this room for?" or "What did I think of last night that I was going to do this morning?" I hear my husband having similar talks outside while looking for tools or planning work projects.

Then there are fruitful minutes of talking to the animals. The cats will sometimes even respond with a muffled meow in their throats, but the Canada geese greet my cheery, "Good morning!" by swimming a short distance away before they return to eat the breakfast corn I have taken to the pond's edge. The birds at the feeder aren't even that sociable. They leave completely when I come to their breakfast table. They do not return until I am safely back in the house or at least in another part of the lawn.

I have been known to speak to our baby trees when I see that they have survived the winter. They give no response to my, "Good for you. You made it!" but at least they don't leave when I am talking to them.

I haven't even mentioned all the possibilities of talking back to the television. Cheering on a team on the tube or beating a comic to the punch line of a joke can be very satisfying, and sputtering in indignation at news commentators who interpret a speech opposite to your view relieves tension.

You can see what a rich, full day we can have as we communicate. Fifty years does not cause word droughts. It merely changes the topic.

Behind the Wheel

We all spend a great deal of time on wheels these days, spending hours in the car daily. Just try going down any main street after school is out, or before it starts in the morning, and you realize that buses are not the only wheels going to and from schools. A drive past any school will show that one of the biggest areas is reserved for parking.

Visualize the old high schools. Can you remember any parking lots? Maybe a few spaces on the street near the building, but there was no problem because very few students drove to school, especially after bus systems were established. Today, streets and parking lots near schools are full all day long, in spite of the fact that school buses deliver and pick up students daily.

Around elementary schools, in addition to the school buses, there is a steady flow of parents picking up children. Many of these parents then drive their offspring to various lessons, ball game practices, appointments, or shopping before heading home. Parents who are not employed outside the home often spend over an hour each day behind the wheel of the family car.

In my childhood family, since we had only one car for two parents and eight children, we seldom used the car alone. We did a lot of walking, and we had the city bus system in Washington, D.C., where we lived in the winter. When I mention this to my children or grandchildren today, their eyes glaze over while they make some sarcastic remark about us walking ten miles to school through hip-deep snow, uphill both ways. Maybe we do tend to exaggerate a bit from time to time, but the truth is, we did survive with only one car in the family, and we did have friends and a social life as well.

In middle age-plus years, one of the hardest blows is to have a doctor or family member say that we should not drive anymore. We have become so closely identified with the independence of having wheels to take us where we want to go, when we want to go, that we feel bereft without this ability.

But there is a bright side. We don't have to go to all those boring meetings. We can sweetly say, "I'd love to come, but you know, I don't drive anymore." We can catch up on all those books we have put off reading until we have more time. Or we can see all our favorite prime-time shows. Maybe we can even get to see every episode of a mini-series for once!

The big trouble is when we reach the stage where we shouldn't drive, we probably can't read too long at a time or watch television very long before falling asleep.

But then that's not too bad either. Sometimes it just seem like it's nicer to nap than to. . . .

Drug Store Fountains

I love chocolate milk shakes. I guess you can tell that by looking at me. But milk shakes of today don't have quite the appeal of the ones I was used to in my youth. Maybe my taste buds have matured along with the rest of me, but I think it is because all that luscious stuff we used --whole milk, cream. Whipped cream toppings are avoided today because we know they aren't good for us.

Even though we can still get a good milk shake, there is something missing when I go by a drive-through window and have a shake handed to me in a paper cup with a lid on it.

I remember walking into Wardin's Drug Store on the north side of the square and sitting either at the counter on stools that revolved (if I tried and I usually did) or, at times, positioning myself farther back in the drug store under the revolving ceiling fans in small, wire-backed chairs at small, round tables. There I was waited on. The ten cent shake, in a tall glass with a straw and a long-handled spoon, was served on a glass plate with two small shortbread-type cookies. We also got what was left in the mixer that wouldn't fit in the glass. If I ordered chocolate soda instead of a milk shake, it came with a swirl of whipped cream and a cherry, complete with stem, on top of the whipped cream. We spent a long time in the coolness of the store, savoring the treat.

Wardin's Drug Store was the first place I ever tasted Dr. Pepper. That was several years before it became a nationwide favorite. We always looked forward to returning to the Midwest each summer where we could order Dr. Pepper.

I wonder if there were a drug store on the square now, would people patronize it as we used to, or would they prefer to drive by and get soft drinks through the car window?

I am planning to drive into Arkansas soon. I think I will stop along the way to get a milk shake to drink as I drive. I hope I can find a quick food place near the highway where I won't have to lose much time. I will have to pay more than a dollar for it. I can dispose of the paper cup at the next stop. My middle age-plus memories will enjoy the refreshment and pretend I'm swiveling on Wardin's Drug Store stool again.

Small Town Choices

Often we hear people say that there is nothing to do in a small town. A recent Saturday night might be a good test of that statement here in Nevada.

We attended a big dinner at the Diner on the Fairgrounds put on by the Farm Bureau for its patrons. This meal was accompanied by a short business meeting, lots of prizes, and a speaker. We had to leave before the speaker was finished because we had tickets to a Rock and Roll concert at Cottey College that was sponsored by the 3M plant.

As we left the Farm Bureau event, we had to drive past the parked cars and traffic for the rodeo held at the arena at the fairground. When we got past the rodeo, we heard the sounds of race cars at the Speedway. From the noise, it sounded like they were having a good attendance.

Driving toward Cottey College, we noticed some late diners entering the back door of a restaurant, and others were gathering to attend one of the three late movies at the Twin Fox theater. Of course, there are always hungry people at Sonic, Hardees, and McDonalds, either eating there or picking up food to eat elsewhere. That night was no exception because we saw many cars at each place.

On the Cottey campus, there was also a dance. Several young people were headed to it.

When we arrived at Haidee and Allen Wild Center for the Performing Arts at the college, we greeted several friends before sitting down to enjoy an evening of music from the 50's, 60's, and 70's. I enjoyed it even though they didn't get back to the really good decade of music—the 40's!

The great thing about the evening was that none of it cost us a penny as businesses were showing appreciation to their clients and the community. The better thing was that at each place we were with people we knew and could visit with while enjoying their company.

The Schell City Festival was also in progress in northeastern Vernon County with all sorts of fun opportunities there.

The variety of entertainment that our area was providing that night should have pleased anyone. If it hadn't, they could have stayed home and watched the last Saturday night of reruns before the new season began. I'm sure there were also neighborhood card parties, family gatherings, and even visiting in the aisles at grocery stores for more informal pleasures.

If I had been in a larger city, I don't know if there would have been anything more appealing to me than the variety offered here. I am quite sure that it would have been more expensive and more stressful getting to the event and finding a parking place. I doubt that I would have found anyone who wanted to visit since I wouldn't expect to find anyone I knew in the audience.

Since we have such good entertainment possibilities on television, the only real advantage I see to going out to an event is being with other people. If these people are stangers that don't want to hear about the trouble I had parking the car or finding the right place to come, then I'd rather just stay home. In Nevada, there are always some people I know (or who know me, but I can't remember who they are).

One of the very good things about Nevada is that had I wanted a more urban entertainment that recent Saturday night, I could have easily driven to Kansas City and still have been home in my own bed at a fairly decent hour, and Joplin offers additional opportunities.

In my middle age-plus years, I find that what I can find to do right here in Nevada or maybe over at Ft. Scott is what pleases me most. In fact, I don't mind often being the one who opts for a night in my lounge chair with *The Dick Van Dyke Show* or reruns of *Murder She Wrote* to keep me company. Or I could try to learn to get on the Internet on my computer! I don't want to appear to be too old and out of touch.

Comfortable Living in the Country

As I was driving to town yesterday, I counted the number of houses I could see from the highway. From our home to the city limits, there were forty-nine homes. I thought back to my childhood, remembering how many homes were on this road then. Several of the former houses are no longer there or have been replaced or remodeled until they do not look the same, but my memory count is much smaller than forty-nine.

Another thing I noticed was that most of the present homes are well cared for with attractive lawns. When I was a child, most of the families in our neighborhood earned their money from their land. They cared for many acres of ground, not just a lawn and a house. Often the barn was in better shape than the house, since the money was earned there.

Today's rural neighbors usually have at least one member working off the farm. In many cases, none of the family has responsibility for more than their one-to-five acres. They devote their agricultural energies to creating a beautiful home place while earning their money elsewhere.

When we live in the country today, we have running water from a rural water district, electricity from the cooperative electric companies, school bus pickup at our drive to good schools in town, telephone connections to the whole world, and television reception equal to none through little satellite dishes.

Now with computers, we can surf the Internet with the rest of the population. In Missouri, roads are now passable in all weather, and few residences are more than a few miles from a paved road.

We can be in town within minutes to get the services of doctors, hospital, business offices, and stores. We have fire protection through our local fire department, and ambulance service is available with or without 911 access.

In my parents' time, there were one-room schools that children walked to, mud roads, local party telephone lines with poor reception, no running water or electricity, and a wintertime air-conditioned outhouse down the path.

It made sense that few chose to live in the country under those conditions when they were making their living in town.

Today country living has most of the benefits of city life and eliminates some of the drawbacks.

No, I don't have land to sell even though I sound like a salesperson. The stigma that used to be associated with living in the country has left enough touchiness that some of us tend to overstate our rural pleasure. I consider Nevada my hometown, even though I don't live within its limits. I take pride in the improvements I see and support as many activities as possible.

When I look out my window and see Canada geese nesting on our pond, and when I see new wheat waving in the wind and know that the land that I see was also walked upon by my father, mother, and grandparents I never knew, I know I will remain just a middle age-plus country girl.

Department Stores

Shopping is on our minds this season. I try to do my shopping locally, but at times I get nostalgic for some stores that are no longer in operation.

The one I miss the most is Moore's Department Store. As a child, I loved to visit Moore's and watch the little wooden cups whizzing by overhead. One cashier was located in the middle of the store in a raised but open office area. A network of wires connected this vantage point with each of the departments in the store. Each wire had a little polished wooden cup, about three inches deep, attached to a metal cap that was secured onto the wire.

As the clerk made a sale, she (or in the shoe department, he) put the sales ticket and money from the customer into this wooden cup, screwed the cup into the metal cap on the wire, and pulled a chain at the sales site to send the cup up the chain to the cashier.

The lofty cashier made change, marked the sales receipt, and sent the missile back to the counter. I can still remember the whirring sound of these transactions that took place far above my head.

On the right, as we entered the store, there was a counter of perfumes and cosmetics. On the left, a long counter was filled with yard goods and materials for sewing.

In the middle of this front part of the store was a square section of counters featuring hosiery, purses, and similar items. A section for baby and small children's clothing on the west wall completed the front section.

Double doors to the west led into the ready-to-wear department where store-bought clothing was available for those lucky enough to have money for such things. A shoe department and a gift shop, featuring crystal and other items, were some of the other departments within the store.

Favorite memories of the little girls in town were the doll boxes that were given to customers who purchased five dollars worth of piece goods. If the customer had a daughter or granddaughter, she received a sturdy white box with blue lettering advertising Moore's store. Inside was a celluloid doll, small pieces of fabric, ribbons, buttons, lace, pins, and other material so that the girl could dress this doll and become interested in sewing.

Girls compared and shared the contents of their boxes since no two were alike. The eight-by-ten-inch box held enough treasures for a child to keep busy for days as she made garments, dressed, undressed, and remade outfits for the little naked doll that was in the middle of the box. There was a side door to Moore's that we liked to use because we could stop at the restrooms or get a drink from the water fountain. We parked in the shade of the trees in the lawn down the street. We then entered by this side door, made our purchases, and returned to our car without too many steps.

This type of store has disappeared from most communities, but isn't it great to have a memory of such a place to shop?

Say Ah!

Last week I had occasion to ride the elevator in the outpatient building of the Nevada Regional Medical Center. That brought back memories because that building to me will always be the old city hospital. One of my children was born there. My parents each were hospitalized there toward the end of their lives, and I visited many friends who were patients there.

Even further back, I remember the old Ammerman Hospital where I was born and where I lost my tonsils. My memories of Dr. Ammerman are somewhat scary. He wore a beard, and when I was fighting the ether for my tonsillectomy, he said that if I took a deep breath, I would grow whiskers like his. That didn't encourage me a bit, and I awoke after the operation afraid that I really did have whiskers on my face! His nurse was, however, comforting and reassuring.

Dr. Ammerman's offices were downstairs with a waiting room off the sidewalk. His examining room was behind the waiting room. There was a big black leather chair similar to a dental chair for patients and a roll-top desk where he did his paperwork. An outside door led to a long flight of stairs up to the hospital on the second floor. There was no elevator, so patients had to be well enough to walk up the stairs or have a very sturdy relative to carry them.

Many doctors have added to the well-being of Vernon County residents. I especially remember Doctors Pascoe and Pearce. Dr. Wray was probably the most talked-about doctor because of his skill as a surgeon, despite the fact that he had several fingers missing from one of his hands. Each doctor evokes special memories.

Today when we go to the clinic established by Dr. Pascoe or cross the street to the Nevada Regional Medical Center, we find specialists, modern equipment of every type, nurses, custodians, cooks, secretaries, business managers, technicians, aides, volunteers, and the ever-present computer.

As I think back to old Dr. Ammerman and his one nurse/cook/helper and thoughtfully rub my chin, I realize now that I am middle age-plus, his prophecy is coming true.

Sure enough, I occasionally find a whisker!

Losing a Good Neighbor

One of the worst things about being middle age-plus is that you begin to out live some of your best friends as well as your family members. People you have known and loved all your life become invalids or die, and you feel a great loss. This happened to many of us this past week when everyone's friend and neighbor, no matter where they lived, died. Opal Hensley, who was geographically our very close neighbor, died on January 24th after we all thought she was making a remarkable recovery from triple bypass surgery. Her death will be felt all over Vernon County, and beyond, because of her talent of being a good neighbor.

Many people felt the warmth of her unexpected gifts of jellies, bread, cookies, and candy. Any person who was facing a hardship or a serious illness would soon see Opal arranging something to bring comfort or relief.

She was the one my mother called when my father died, and she stayed with her until I could get home. She arranged for other helps from neighbors and made the whole ordeal much easier for our entire family. She had earlier driven for my father or both of my parents wherever they needed to go after they were no longer able to drive and no family member was nearby.

When my sister Miriam returned to live in the family home, Opal became her close friend and supplied a feeling of family until, and after, Lester and I returned to live here ourselves.

When she was working at Ramey's bakery and we were home for a visit with our grandchildren, Opal presented them with cookies as we shopped or stopped for a quick visit.

None of our family ever returned for a visit without wanting to go see the Hensleys because they were part of being home. Since Opal was two years old, her family had lived in the house just down the road. Her father, Jim Berry, and my father, Chester Gray, were such good friends that when Mr. Berry died, my father returned from Washington, D.C., on the train to attend his funeral.

The first shivaree I ever attended was the one for Opal and Bill. And I was at their fiftieth wedding anniversary and all the years in between. In the 1950s, when Lester was with the University Extension office and we lived on this road, Opal and I became even closer friends. Since our children were about the same age, we spent many a pleasant morning letting the kids play while we visited. She made a lamb birthday cake for our son Mark's first birthday and took Michael to Sunday School with her family when our daughter Shirley was having eye surgery.

These are small things I have mentioned, but

these small things happened so often that they became a part of our lives together.

In recent years, since we have returned to live again as neighbors, our friendship has deepened even more because of sharing church associations, club affiliations, facing illness and death of our older siblings. We share pride and joy that our families extended even to great-grandchildren and from the great comfort of having a life-long friend that understands and accepts you just as you are.

I deeply regret that I never told Opal what she meant to me. I hope she realized it. I had the pleasure of being her secret sister in club this past year and had decided to make it a special time. She didn't guess my identity but told me how much she had enjoyed my monthly tokens.

As we cherish the last jar of the homemade jelly she gave us for Christmas, I think of all the goodies the church and the community will miss, but the biggest loss will not be her excellent cooking but her loving concern for everyone she knew.

Those of us who were Opal's friends have been blessed. As we share the loss, we will try to continue her tradition by becoming more like our friend and being the best neighbor we can be. In honor of Opal Hensley, I plan to start telling more of my friends what they mean to me, not only in words but also in acts of thoughtfulness.

Good neighbors are a gift from God. We had one of the best.

Hardware Stores

During a recent lunch break, I took a leisurely walk around the square, admiring the attractive window displays and flower tubs brightening the streets. I began to think back to how the square looked when I was a child. One memory jumps out at me because I could never understand what it meant.

At each of the open stairways to apartments and offices above the ground level store was a big sign that read, "Do Not Expectorate On The Stairs." Later when I understood what it meant, I was still puzzled. Anyone uncouth enough to spit on the stairs probably didn't know what *expectorate* meant! Now staircases shut off with a door at the bottom, so I can't tell if the signs are still there.

To the best of my memory, the only building that houses the same business or office that it did in the 1930s is First National Bank. At least none of the places that I was interested in as a child are still there.

One of the mysterious places on the square was Johannes Hardware Store. This store was a big attraction to me. As I entered the store, two different worlds opened up. To the right was a breath-taking display of glassware, crystal, delicate ornaments, gifts in all price ranges, and two helpful women, the Johannes sisters, to guide me to a selection. (I now realize they were also concerned that my childhood excitement about the store offerings might cause breakage.) They treated me, even as a child, as a valued customer and never made me feel unwelcome.

To the left of the front door was the hardware section. There, resting on the oiled wooden floors, were kegs of nails and screws, hammers, saws, and all tools necessary for building or repairs.

Nothing was prepackaged, but was taken from the shelves with metal scoops, tongs, or by the helpful owner who counted out the exact amount of nails needed. A rolling ladder helped him climb to the top shelves to get the merchandise stored clear to the ceiling. The odor of oiled hardware, sweeping compound, and wooden floors blended with the more delicate odors from the north side gift shop offerings. I think I could still identify where I was if the scene could be recreated today and my nose had a chance to relive that scent.

I wonder if children today will wax nostalgic about pushing a shopping cart through a discount store as I have about this memory of personalized shopping. Time brings changes, and the square has different attractions, but I'm glad my memory lets me enjoy the fun of hardware stores.

The Old Neighborhood Today

The popular saying "It takes a village to raise a child" is very true. However, I have decided that there is another truism for our age-group. That is "It takes a neighborhood to nurture a middle age-plus person." The older I get, the more I cherish my friendships of the past and present. Those friendships have not all occurred in a geographic area called a neighborhood, but many of them are centered in several square miles from our present home, which is also the neighborhood of my half-time childhood home.

When I walk or drive down familiar roads and wave to the people living in the homes along the way, I also mentally wave to the people who used to live nearby. Often there is not even a home site present anymore, but I can vividly see Mrs. Eaton out with her canna flowers, Mrs. Horn looking out the window from her platform rocker by the party line phone, or Mrs. Watson walking across the railroad track to get the mail that Mildred Eaton brought up to her from the corner. The Watson home has been replaced by a third generation neighbor Gordon Halcomb who, with his wife, has established their home site in this familiar spot not far from where his parents and grandparents raised their families. The Horn farm now belongs to my husband and me, and new neighbors live in a new home where the Eatons used to live.

These details don't mean much to those who didn't know these people, but they do illustrate not only how neighborhoods change but how the spirit of the area can remain.

We had an exciting day in our neighborhood last week, and all of us turned out to watch the goings on. The old Franks' house was being moved down the road to make room for the granddaughter and grandson-in-law of the Walter Franks to build a new home on the original home site. What makes it even more exciting is that the great-granddaughter and her family will be moving into the old house in its new location. When we go down the road, where for the last few years different renters had been our neighbors, we will now see two generations of one of the old neighborhood families living in new or remodeled homes.

I was surprised at how happy this made me. When we retired back to my original home setting, I was looking forward to renewing friendships with all my old neighbors. This has happened, and we have enjoyed many pleasant visits with our old friends, but our years have taken a toll and some important links began to be missed. The death of Opal Hensley left a big gap in the neighborhood, following the deaths of Elmer and Ruby O'Toole and even younger neighbors like Roger Tyer. It looked like the old gang was quickly disappearing and our dreams of spending our retirement days among old friends would be altered.

But the arrival of two generations of an old family reminded me that the neighborhood will change, but it will still be a neighborhood that nurtures those within it. There will still be persons who know your name, are ready to lend a hand when you need it, and who will wave merrily as they pass by.

It doesn't have to be the same beloved friends to continue the feeling of neighborliness. Even if we have to reestablish ourselves in some other type of living arrangements, we can still bask in a spirit of friendship in whatever new neighborhood we find ourselves.

Wherever we will be, we can still have the memories of the old neighborhood. And it is really a good feeling to know that the old neighborhood will still have some of the same old names for years to come.

That house being moved down the road brought us all together to watch the progress, but it also brings hope for the future of the nurturing community we call home.

Parallel Parking

One of the best things about having a square as the middle of a business district is that I don't have to leave my car in a parallel parking space. The lined spaces heading into the curb or the spaces in the middle of the street are much easier to use than parallel parking spaces.

One of the biggest hurdles that one taking a driving test has to face is the parking test. When my mother was middle age-plus, she had to take the driving test because she let her license expire. She told the trooper that he might as well skip that part, for she wouldn't be able to pass the test.

I can and do park parallel, but I don't enjoy it, especially if I have an audience. When I go to the newspaper office, I have to park parallel. If it is break time for the employees at W.F. Norman Company next door, I am tempted to drive on by, go back to park on the square, and walk to the newspaper office. Trying to squeeze into a parking place while six or eight men are leaning against the wall with nothing better to do than watch me is not my idea of fun.

And if I have helpful passengers in the car, it is also unsettling to try to maneuver into a tight spot.

Those giving directions often use a different method in their own vehicles, and their directions add to my stress.

Parking parallel on the left side of a one-way street is even harder for me. My driving instincts are all geared to the right side, and trying to reverse this for left-handed parking doesn't come easy.

I wonder about parking problems when my parents were young adults and drove a horse and wagon or buggy to town. I suppose they tied Old Nell to a hitching post around the courthouse square. I never heard about any problems of finding space to tie the horse, but I can imagine that on Saturdays the square could get quite full with horses and buggies. There are not many left who were adults in those days. I would love to hear from those who do remember. I have lots of questions.

One of the first questions is who cleaned up the streets after several horses were tied to hitching posts for an hour or so?

I know there were watering tanks for the animals, but were they on the square or in another part of town? Did the horses ever get into fights with one who was tied nearby?

And finally, were there traffic rules for those in horse and buggy when going around the square, or could they go anywhere they wanted?

There are people today who were small children in the horse and buggy time. Often they forget details, but some of us can remember details of our childhood better than adults of that time could. Certainly, we can remember those details easier than we recall what happened yesterday!

So maybe I can get my questions answered.

9

Family Is Forever

The guy who wasn't smart enough to marry my daughter is the parent of the smartest grandchild in the world.

Joey Adams

A Bond Between Generations

One of our recent Christmas pictures shows our two small great-granddaughters Shelbie and Marilyn sitting side by side on the piano bench pounding out a tune. Above them are pictures of their parents and grandparents at various ages, plus numerous uncles, aunts, and cousins. Then a special picture on the wall shows my grandmother as a young woman.

This picture brought to mind the great gift we middle age-plus people have of being the bridge between many generations. In my case, six generations have I known, loved, and learned from. My grandmother died when I was in kindergarten, but I remember her gooseberry pies, the big house in Stanberry, Missouri, and the fun of visiting Grandma and Grandpa each summer.

Today, I have great-grandaughters. Perhaps they will remember that I never in my life made a gooseberry pie but hopefully that it was fun to come visit.

My grandmother and mother were ladies in the true sense of the word. Even though my kids, grandkids, and great-grandkids will probably not use that term to describe me, I know there is much of each of these two women in my makeup, even if it doesn't always show. I see some of those same traits clear into this sixth generation of my female relatives. (The same would be true for the male side, but since I am the one writing, I can tell it from my side!)

Part of eternal life is the heritage we give to those who follow, and part of our gift of life comes from the influence that came to us from our ancestors. Even though both my mother and grandmother made wonderful gooseberry pies and I do not, I still reap the benefit of knowing that gifts of love—from the oven or from participation in young lives—will remain forever in the family.

Maybe sitting on a cold bleacher cheering for a beloved player can bring as warm a memory as a warm pie. Perhaps a long car trip to share a special event can mean as much as frying chickens.

When I finally get around to organizing my snapshots from the last twenty years, I will clearly see again that family is forever, and those blessed with good ancestors can always be grateful.

Hopefully, those two young pianists will someday remember and appreciate a great-grandmother that loved them very much.

Happy Birthday, Miriam

The other day was my sister Miriam's ninetieth birthday. It boggles my mind to think that she could be that age. I remember when she became twenty-five. My brothers teased her about being a quarter of a century old. I thought that was very old. Now that I join her as middle age-plus, I don't feel that ninety is really all that old, but it is getting close to a century mark (which is her goal), and that does inspire me.

Miriam graduated from Cottey College in Nevada, Missouri, a few days before I was born, so she wasn't home to be part of our household on a regular basis in my childhood. When she was there, it was always a special time—a holiday or a summer vacation. When I was in grade school, she was an elementary teacher. She moved to junior high teaching about the time I reached that age. This was a matter of pride and concern for me. Often Miriam tried to teach my sister Ellen and me what she was teaching her students. It didn't work. We resisted. That is probably why I never became a good dancer. Physical education, and especially dance, were the subjects Miriam taught. After getting her doctorate, she became a college professor about the time that I was in college.

Now that we are each retired and living as neighbors again, she is the teacher of my age group, and I resist learning. In spite of myself, she is teaching me about handling the aging process. This time I am an unwilling student, not because of clumsiness or stubbornness, but because I don't want my sister to be getting old.

Miriam is the oldest of eight; I am the youngest. Five of my siblings are over eighty. I'm not ready for that. I want those brothers and sisters who are my lifetime idols to remain as they are in my memory. I know that cannot be; therefore, I object to being shown how to age gracefully.

When I was the director of The Neighbors, I could enjoy the participants and be inspired by them. But it is different when it is a sister. Parents are expected to get old. Other people naturally will get old. But brothers and sisters are made of the same stuff as I am, and when they get older, it hurts more.

I want to be able to gather on a moonlit lawn and run and play. I don't want to leave those days.

Miriam is a good teacher. She has shown me that life can be enjoyed very much even if you can't dance or play games on the lawn. She has shown me that interest in what is going on in the world and in the community can remain keen, even if some of it is experienced through television instead of through world travels. She has shown me that enjoyment of pets and family can replace the honors of high achievements professionally, and that even though we didn't share day by day experiences that the bonds of sisters remain close in spite of changes we don't welcome.

Happy Birthday, Miriam. Keep on teaching us, even if we balk.

Too Many Bosses

I had always thought that when I reached middle age-plus that I could be my own boss and make my own decisions about most things in my life. Being the youngest child in a big family, I constantly had someone telling me what to do, or more often, telling me what not to do that I had already done.

Ellen, who is the sister closest to my age, had a good friend who lived nearby in Washington, D.C. Her family was much more formal than ours, and mealtimes there were a lesson in elegance. Her father carved the meat at the table and filled our plates and handed them to us. With the number around the table in our own family, that would have taken all night and cut down on the merriment too much for our tastes. But it was great to experience this other lifestyle through these gracious people who invited us over often.

On the short walk home, Ellen told me all the things that I had done wrong. I think she was trying to avoid future embarrassment for herself as the big sister, but our friends never gave me any hint that I had breached a rule of etiquette. I was so used to being told what to do that I didn't worry about these episodes too much, though I still remember them over sixty years later!

As I grew older, I felt I was taking more control of my life. The older siblings married or moved away, and I had less bosses at home, but I had a whole new set of family members that I wanted to impress as we gained in-laws and later nieces and nephews. I wanted those young relatives to look up to me, so I tried very hard to gain their respect and affection.

After marriage, I was not only influenced by my husband's wishes and needs but also a whole new family by marriage entered the picture. Since my background was different from most of theirs, it took some adjusting, on both sides, as we learned from each other.

One example is the story Lester tells often about the different styles of gravy. My family served roast beef regularly on Sundays, so my parents could go to church while the roast was safely cooking in the oven. The gravy was made from the meat drippings in the roast pan, with flour and a small amount of water mixed together to thicken the gravy. Lester's family fried most of their meat, and the gravy was made in the frying pan, with flour stirred into the fat and milk added to the flour/grease mixture.

Although my mother also made that kind of gravy for breakfast when we had bacon or sausage, Lester remembers the Sunday dinners more clearly and has remarked that when you marry into a family, you marry into their gravy. As our children arrived with their demands and needs, my activities stretched to support each of their interests. And, of course, the natural sequence happens again, and we are enlarged by in-laws, grandchildren, and the other families of each of these. This is a blessing, and I wouldn't want it to be diminished in any way, but once in a while, since I have reached middle age-plus, I feel that I should be pleasing just myself.

This week a family member told me that I should start cutting back on my activities. The activities I want to cut back on are things like housecleaning and cooking. I enjoy the other things too much to cut back. I want to visit my friends from towns where we have lived in the past. I want to go see my siblings and their families more often. I want to spend time just sitting and watching the sun reflect from the pond outside our windows. Most of all, I want to be the person each of these loved ones wants me to be. Psychologists would have a heyday with me, wouldn't they?

I've reached a place where I don't let it bother me too much. In this gained tranquility, yesterday I got ready to take my five-year-old great-granddaughter up to the road to meet the school bus at 7:10 a.m. I left my hair in pincurls so that the dewy morning wouldn't give me a bad hair day. I put a robe on over my p.j's and was ready to get in the car to drive to the main road. Marilyn took one look at me and said she didn't want me going up there looking like that. I promised I wouldn't get out of the car, and since it was too dark for anyone to see me inside the car, she relented.

Another generation has made itself heard! When I am far enough down the road of middle age-plus plus, perhaps I will be able to make my own decisions? I doubt it. The nurses will then tell me what to do!

Here Comes the Bride

I have attended many weddings in my life. The first one was my sister Kathryn's wedding in our home in Washington, D.C. Ellen and I were honored to be involved by forming a ribbon aisle for the bride to follow from the stairway to the bay window where the ceremony took place. I was wearing a frilly dress with a wide skirt. As I turned the corner from the stair landing, I got entangled with the ribbon. It didn't mar the wedding, but my eleven-year-old emotions couldn't hold back the tears later when Kathryn began to tell the family goodbye before their get-away.

Emotions are just under the surface at most weddings. The gaiety of the occasion can't mask a change in family relationships which causes sadness even in the midst of happiness. Other weddings in our family didn't have quite the emotional impact of this one that took the first sibling away from home.

We two younger sisters also formed a ribbon aisle for another sister, Gertrude, who got married in the back lawn of our Washington home. Later, when I got married, we had Kathryn's children, along with their cousins, form a ribbon aisle for my father to march me down in the lawn of our farm home. We were fortunate to be able to celebrate our golden Anniversary on that same lawn but without any ribbon aisles. However, we did have grandchildren and great-grandchildren present who had a much better time playing in a porch swing than they would have had making a formal aisle.

My husband had the honor of performing the wedding ceremony for several of our family members. Children, grandchildren, a nephew, and many close friends have chosen Lester to be the minister at their ceremony. Not long ago he was privileged to perform the wedding for a grandson in Quincy, Illinois.

These family ceremonies have special meanings, but some of the most memorable weddings were those of couples we did not know very well. Some were very formal, but others quite informal. One groom didn't even bother to put on his shoes.

So far he hasn't had any weddings scheduled where the bride or groom did not show up, but often there have been last minute changes in songs, singer, musicians, or attendants. In spite of nerves, most weddings do go smoothly and no one but the immediate wedding party knows of the near crises that occur.

Since Lester has been a minister for over thirty-five years, we have been able to observe that the type of wedding has little effect on the longevity of the marriage. Some of the most lavish weddings did not keep the marriage intact for more than a few years. Some simple ceremonies, with just a couple standing up with the bride and groom, have begun a family that is still living happily ever after (or close to it).

Concerns about dress, style, numbers of guests, type of reception, handling of gifts, ordering flowers or cake, all add stress to the happy couple and their parents. Often the father of the bride proclaims that he will buy a ladder for his other daughters, so they can elope rather than have another big wedding. However, he is usually beaming with pride as he comes down the aisle with his daughter.

My middle age-plus emotions are not quite as evident as my tears at my big sister's wedding, but no matter who is getting married, I find a lump in my throat at some time in the ceremony. Often the lump comes when I see the parents of the couple reach for each other's hands when the young couple repeats the vows. Then I pray that these newlyweds will have the same love for each other in the future that these parents show by their simple act.

Not Much of a Cook

At a recent club meeting, our roll call was a favorite dish our mothers made. In this group of sixteen women, everyone began their answer with the phrase "My mother was an excellent cook...." Or "Everything my mother made was good..." Since most of the members are either middle age or middle age-plus (except two lucky members whose mothers were also at the meeting), they were speaking about a woman who lived and cooked many years ago.

This conversation made me wonder. Were all the women of the past better cooks than the women of today, or do all children remember their mothers as good cooks regardless of their real skill? The nearest I come to a good cook is when Darlene Tweten's Kitchen Chatter is printed on the same page as my column. But surprisingly, from time to time, I hear one of my children or grandchildren ask how I prepared a certain dish they remembered. But I'm sure there have been very few times when one of my children requested something like Mother used to make. I served blackened chicken years before I knew that this was a Louisiana delicacy. I thought it was careless cooking. I taught my children that good Cream of Wheat had lots of nice lumps in it. My homemade bread came from the neighbors or sympathetic church members, and pies have always been a lost cause with me.

If my children ever have to answer such a roll call, I am not sure what they would answer.

My birth family is compiling a mealtime memory book which will include recipes from four generations as well as memories of meal times. When I thought of what my entry could be, I found that I was remembering the social aspect more than the actual food. I vividly remember the seating arrangements, the give and take among my siblings, and the long discourses my father provided at the table. But most of all, I remember the feelings of belonging, enjoying one another's company, and knowing that supper was always at six. If you weren't there, then my mother put a plate in the oven.

I wonder if this same type of memory among middle age-plus folks isn't what makes our mothers seem like such good cooks? We all sat together at the table with no radio or television to distract. We knew what to expect and when to expect it. We also knew that the total family had to be considered over any one person's erratic schedule.

Many families today have about three evening meals—for those who come home early and have to leave soon, for those who come home late, and for those in between. Many do not sit at a table together except on rare occasions.

And often the television is a big part of mealtime.

Family is more important than exellent meals. My kids may forget my poor cooking while they remember that we sat at the table together ...whether they wanted to or not!

Goodbye, Miriam

Every Thursday for three years my sister Miriam had cut out my column and put it in a file folder marked, *Carolyn's Columns.* She was not able to do this last week, nor any future weeks, as she died last Wednesday morning. I had written two columns in advance because of a busy schedule coming up, but I have postponed using those so I can write a more suitable one for her today.

On her ninetieth birthday last November, I did write a column about her and our relationship. She was pleased with it, and I am very glad that I did that while she was able to enjoy it.

This column, however, is more for me than for her. When your oldest sibling dies, especially when there is the age difference that we had (twenty years), it is almost like losing a parent all over again. I have never known life without her, even though many years we were not close together geographically. There was always the reality of this big sister who was such a force in our family.

Her personality controlled any gathering she was in, and she certainly tried to control her younger sisters! She never married or had a family of her own, but she always had time to be concerned about her brothers and sisters and later her nieces and nephews. She faithfully recognized our birthdays and other special events and made sure that she visited in each of our homes throughout the years to keep in close touch.

In spite of our age difference, we had the opportunity to be neighbors for the past eight years and belong to various local organizations together. We shared our interest in nature, our friends, and animals, especially cats.

Although her last weeks were not too comfortable, she continued to enjoy watching the birds that found her tiny bird feeder by her new apartment. On her last day, she was able to get excited about the unexpected October snowfall; she had fun with her preschool care-giver Audrey Daniels who had become a real friend. She was also happy to learn about my honor as Business and Professional Women's Woman of the Year.

After a restless night, she dozed off toward dawn and died in her sleep as the new day appeared. Our family is very grateful for the help of all the Hospice workers and the friends who shared the care-giving responsibilities.

We all have regrets for little things we wish we had done when a loved one or a friend dies, but I know Miriam felt the love and respect of her family, friends, and community and was happy that she returned to her hometown for her last days. Thanks for sharing these days with her and with me.

Cooking from Scratch Lives On

My brother Harold was here recently for a visit to his hometown. I was very proud to know that this big brother, who's eighteen years older than I, could travel alone to Sacramento, California, for a four-day jazz festival, stop off to visit his two little sisters in Missouri, return to his home in Washington, D.C., and feel better than he had when he left home. Four days of listening to jazz would probably wear me down very quickly, but he has always been a fan of jazz, even when it was considered a slightly sinful type of music.

During his visit, we had the fun of visiting old haunts and showing off new things to him. We especially enjoyed showing the new library and museum and visiting the old museum/jail where he often visited as a youth—not as a prisoner, but as a friend of the sheriff. He was quite pleased with his old hometown and the progress it has made.

One of the things that interested me the most was a luncheon in Kansas City with his grandson and wife on our way to take him to the airport.

This young couple, first-time home owners, were anxious to share the delight of suburban life with us. Our niece talked about their garden and her cooking, explaining that she cooked everything from scratch. She asked Ellen and me for gardening and cooking tips.

While we were pleased at the happiness this couple showed, we sisters hid our amusement. It has been years since we had cooked from scratch. Our age places us, in her eyes, in the old school, but we're too busy to spend much time in the kitchen or in a garden. Meals on the run are just as common for us as for those fifty years younger.

My appetite for home-grown foods is keen, but can be satisfied by some quick visits to the Farmer's Market. Frozen foods, using the microwave, and packaged salads do very nicely.

I tried to remember how I viewed those who were our age when I was the age of this young woman. I suppose I thought they knew everything about cooking, housework, and child care. I wonder if they smiled at my attempts to learn or to prove that I had learned the art of home-making? This delightful couple painted a rosy picture of their new life. I hope they don't try too hard.

They had a good model in grandfather Harold who takes time to enjoy life at an age when many would be afraid to travel. Hopefully, they will also live to enjoy a ninth decade, but I'll bet she won't be cooking from scratch if she does.

Immortality of a Family Lawn

I have decided that one of the longest lasting indicators of immortality is a family lawn. I am in charge of mowing the lawn of our family home. It is a beautiful spot with many, many memories in every corner. As I run our tractor mower over the large expanse, I find myself remembering all those who have worked to preserve this place for the present generation.

I have not heard in detail what the lawn looked like when my parents bought the place in 1905, but early pictures show that at least part of the lawn was cut short and without weeds. Twenty years later when I entered the picture, the lawn was very much as it is today, except one corner was the garden spot and another was the orchard.

Our move to Washington, D.C., during the school year made gardening impractical, and the apple trees eventually died of old age. My brothers turned the garden spot into a crude miniature golf course for a couple of summers, but after that, it was incorporated into the complete lawn.

Each of my siblings has spent hours grooming this garden spot. My mother loved to trim around the fence posts and trees in the late evenings.

She did not tolerate weeds in the lawn or trash and leaves on the sidewalk.

Many others have also shared in the care of this lawn. Neighbor boys and men cut it in the spring before the family arrived home. Farm managers and hired hands have all shared this chore.

Now it is my job. I look at the thriving blue-grass and the pesky crab grass (which we used to mispronounce and mortify our brother-in-law). I duck under massive limbs of cedars that have withstood all the years of my life, and I fight similar gopher hills that my parents and others deplored.

Then in sadness, I realize that many of those who have shared this beautification task with me are either no longer living or no longer have the ability to do such a chores, but the lawn is still there. The trees are still there. The memories have outlived many of us and hopefully will out live me. In middle age-plus years, I am doing all I can to preserve this spot of immortality.

It's raining today. That means the lawn will soon need mowing again. I will share the task in memory with all those who made it possible for me to be the present caretaker of a heritage.

I will silently thank each one and hope they are not watching if I don't trim close to every tree or if a spot or two gets cut a little too close.

Space on This Earth

I'm very glad that my parents did not raise their family in these days when the world is concerned with overpopulation. I know that is a very legitimate problem and one I am concerned about. When I was a child, the fact that I was one of a family of eight children was a matter of pride to me. Every time I entered our home it was like going to a party.

My oldest brother Harold, who recently celebrated his ninetieth birthday, didn't marry until he was nearly thirty years old. He used to say that he was having too much fun at home. I imagine the Depression had something to do with it.

Eight children over a span of twenty years, each with best friends or romantic interests who visited, often brought quite a few people in the house. Each of us had our own little space in a bedroom we shared, but I don't remember that being any great concern. We never knew the possibility of closing a door for privacy, except in the bathroom, and that was rather iffy sometimes.

When I visualize the ten of us using the one bathroom on the second floor of our home in Washington, I try to remember how we managed. I vividly remember taking a bath while watching one of my older sisters washing her hair in the bathroom sink. I also remember one time when I was very glad that part of our basement floor was not cemented over. At that time, an aunt and uncle were visiting, and my uncle didn't realize the urgency of small girls.

Mealtimes were a riot and even washing dishes was fun because one of my sisters (never a brother!!) washed while I dried. After supper, my father listened to the radio in the living room while he read the evening paper and *Time* magazine. My mother joined him, because after the meal was on the table, she was through. I alternated between hanging out in my older sisters' room, and watching all the glamorous things these young ladies did, and playing on the living room floor with my dolls.

I can't remember being alone in the house for even a few minutes until I was in high school and the older siblings had left home. I sometimes went up on the smokehouse roof or into the branches of the Jonathan apple tree to meditate and be alone but soon worried I was missing out on something and came down.

Some of my biggest decisions came when a couple of my siblings went somewhere in the car while the rest were still at home. I loved to GO PLACES, but I was also afraid something might happen at home while I was gone.

I hope the world hasn't suffered because of the over-population of our family. I know my middle age-plus memories rejoice in each incident I recall of growing up with seven brothers and sisters. Hopefully, we have made good use of our space on this crowded earth.

10

The Rules Are Changing

You have brains in your head.
You have feet in your shoes.
You can steer yourself
Any direction you choose.

Dr. Seuss

Old Houses Need Respect

When we reach middle age-plus, we begin to lose some of our good friends. Each loss leaves a gap and causes us to appreciate the many friends that are still around.

Another loss we experience is losing a familiar old house in the neighborhood. In our mind's eye, we travel certain roads and see the former homes that housed our friends and neighbors. Then we drive or walk down an often traveled road to find that the house is gone. This happened in our neighborhood when the old Post house was taken down. The area that had been lawn and barnyard was leveled for crops. The only reminders of the old homestead are a couple of cedar trees near the road.

When I remember our immediate neighborhood, I can think of many homesteads that are completely gone. There is no sign left that at one time a family lived there with a lawn, garden, barns, and a house. Only a memory remains that this was the old Truskett place or one of many other names.

We farm right over the spot where Mrs. Horn used to hang out her wash. Only increased fertility in a few spots indicates where the barnyard, outhouse, and chicken yards once stood.

We feel sad as we think about our own beloved homes and wonder about the future for them. A much sadder sight is the homestead that deteriorates because of neglect. There are several of those in our neighborhood, and although I understand the reluctance of families to tear down the old home place, it's much better than letting it fall down or become a haven for varmints.

An old house is similar to an older woman. When there is light in her eyes (windows) and open arms (doors) to greet the remaining family members or guests, she is still beautiful and to be treasured. When the light is gone, and the arms can no longer reach out in greeting, we bury the body with honor and love.

An old house needs the same respect. When it is no longer any use for a family, we need to let it go as we do the remains of a beloved person.

I applaud the Post family in their decision to give their old home place a decent burial and let the land be used for growing crops. As we pass the area, we can still think back to remember those tall blond boys, girls, men, and women busily taking care of daily chores and adding their good influence to the community.

But I still sorta miss the place as I take the back road to Moundville.

Stuck in the Mud Together

I think I might have been a gypsy in another life because I am fascinated with roads. I always want to see where they go.

After attending a meeting on Happy Hollow Road recently, I headed home over a road that eventually became gravel. It was very dusty, and, at times, when I met a car, the dust was so thick I had to stop for a moment before I could continue driving. At first, I wondered how the people who lived in the nice houses on this road could stand all that dust; then I realized that every house was tightly shut up with air conditioning inside. The families were not subject to dust and other annoyances that I remember fighting.

The one thing that was worse than dust on the back roads was mud. If we were away from home when it started to rain, we immediately ran for the car to get home. If we waited too long, we faced the possibility of driving first on a slippery dirt road, as the rain began, and then a little later in just plain mud.

The first car through after the rain had the biggest problem. The ruts made by the first driver remained for everyone else to follow, or avoid, until dry weather or another rain altered the situation. If we saw that the first car had made it through with no places where footprints or splashed mud showed that the car had gotten stuck, then our best bet was to get in the ruts and follow them. That was like driving at Worlds of Fun where steel barriers keep the cars within the boundaries. We controlled the speed, but the rut did the guiding after we committed the wheels into its path.

If the first car, or some subsequent car, had gotten stuck, the trick was to avoid the ruts by driving between them. That also took some careful maneuvering because the ruts acted like a magnet, pulling the car into its clutches. If the rain continued, the road stayed slippery and rutty. If the windshield wipers didn't work well, we knew we might as well start taking off our shoes because someone would have to get out and push.

Since I was the smallest, I often had the dubious honor of guiding the car while those with bigger muscles did the pushing. But I would have rather pushed than face the wrath of my brothers when I let the car slip back into the ruts after they had pushed it out of trouble.

When human power was not enough to get a car out of the mud, we had to use either horses or tractors to pull the car out. Naturally, since this help wasn't just standing there waiting for a job, someone had to take a long walk to the nearest neighbor for help.

Today's weather reporters on radio or television often bemoan the possibility of rain that might spoil a weekend. As badly as most summer rains are needed for the growing things, today's weather people have no idea how rains in the past could not only spoil a weekend's activities but an entire family's relationship when they were stuck in the mud together.

There is nothing like caked mud between your toes, on your face, and all over your new outfit to make you irritable.

Vernon County today has almost no mud roads. The good old days can keep this memory with no regrets from me. I'll explore many roads, but I'm comfortable knowing that I'll have a firm foundation under my wheels the next time I venture out.

Cloakrooms

Whatever happened to cloakrooms? I am sure that many of my readers have fond, or not so fond, memories of cloakrooms at their elementary schools. When we got to junior high or high school, it was a big thing to have a locker--with a combination lock no less. The fears I had that I would forget my combination or not know how to use it were lessened by practices at home with sister Ellen. With an old lock we had for our bicycles, she drilled me how to go past the first number the first time, then return to stop on the first number, reverse my direction to the second number, and reverse again until the third number opened the lock. The pride I felt in performing this function smoothly on my first day of junior high was equal to many bigger triumphs in later life.

Before these heady days of lockers, we had cloakrooms. In our school in Washington, D.C., the cloakroom was a long narrow storage room with open doors at each end. The designated "In" door allowed us to all go the same direction as we removed our coats or sweaters and hung them on a preassigned hook, placed our lunch pail on the shelf right above our hook, and deposited either rubbers, galoshes, or roller skates (depending on the weather) on the floor below our hook. We exited the "Out" door to take our books to our desk.

A few sissy-type students carried a book satchel. This was not like the book bags of today. Constructed of a combination of fabric and leather, it was a narrow carrying case with two buckles to fasten the flap which closed the bag. One handle was on the top for carrying. In our school, the only ones who carried such an accessory were the very studious, show-off types. Today's students would call them *nerds*. We didn't have that term then.

Even though those bags could have been very helpful, most of us preferred to carry our books at waist level, resting on our hip bone with one arm holding them in place. A few boys used a strap around the books and carried them over their shoulders or swinging at the end of their arms.

At our desks, we were required to have everything inside except what we were working on at the time. Nothing could be on the floor except our feet.

Cloakrooms had other uses, too. The child being punished was often banished to a seat in the cloakroom. That treatment didn't give the student the public humiliation of being seated in the hall but did allow the teacher to observe the student during the exile.

I'm sure there were lights in the cloakrooms, but in my memory they were always dark. Before going home, I remember rows of us sitting on the floor pulling on our galoshes. Since most of us walked to school, or at least walked several blocks to a city bus line, many times of the year we had to wear some shoe covering. This wet rubber footwear became rather aromatic as several pairs warmed in the heated cloakroom. Some boys tried to get by with leaving their galoshes on during the day. Most teachers would not permit this. I remember our fifth grade teacher Mrs. Knowlton lecturing us on the evils of getting our feet too warm with the galoshes on and then going outside. I still hear the threat in her voice as she described what might befall us if we did not heed her warnings.

Country schools usually had an anteroom away from the classroom proper where the students left their wraps and lunches. Some of them actually had a cloakroom, but almost all had either a separate room or at least a wall on one side of the classroom with hooks for storage.

In our town's shiny, modern schools today, elementary students drape coats over chair backs. Evidently fear of head lice makes some parents or students prefer to use the backs of their chairs.

Head lice are not new, so I suppose this was always a threat, but I never heard of head lice as I was growing up. Therefore, I can assume that I never contracted them from my years of keeping my coat and hat in a cloakroom, and my coat tail didn't get muddy from other students walking on the hem as it hung from my chair!

V-J Day

One advantage of being middle age-plus is that when special anniversaries come along in our history, we can remember the event ourselves. The flood of the fifty-years-ago recognitions having to do with the end of World War II is a good example.

I can vividly remember the end of the war. I was living in a rooming house for the summer term at the University of Missouri. Lester lived in a rooming house nearby. We were not married yet. He had come by so we could walk to a restaurant to buy our supper. I was sitting on the porch of my rooming house when he arrived. Suddenly, bells began ringing all over town and cars hit the streets with horns blaring. This was before television. I didn't have my radio on, as I was studying for finals, but it didn't take long for us to learn the cause of the celebration.

Those who were passing in the streets started yelling, "The war is over. Japan has surrendered." We joined the crowds milling in the streets and went up to Broadway where hundreds of people of all ages, but mainly college students, were walking, running, driving cars, or just standing and watching. Horns, bells, and other noise makers kept the air full of sound. Those in the crowd added their voices to the din.

I don't remember if we ever ate supper or not, but when the crowd began to show evidence of too much celebration by using alcohol, we returned to my rooming house and listened to the radio in the parlor. We had no concept at the time of what an atom bomb was or what it would mean for generations to come. We just knew that the war was over, and we were happy.

Other members of my family had different experiences of the war's ending. My sister Kathryn was vacationing with her family in a park in Indiana. They didn't have their radio on, and when they went to eat at the lodge for supper, no one mentioned anything about the news. They did not know what happened until the next day.

It's hard to realize in this present age of instant communication that within the lifetimes of many of our citizens, news did not get around for days or even weeks.

What is even harder for me to realize is that people I consider my peers--as we work together in the community--were not even alive when these events happened. At times, I will comment on something that seems fairly recent to me. When I am answered with a blank stare or a slight smile, I remember that this really happened twenty, thirty, or forty years ago.

My peers cannot begin to know what memories I am recalling. So all of you middle age-plus friends, what were you doing when World War II ended? Many of you were in uniform and had great reasons for celebration. Others were waiting for husbands, brothers, or sons to come home from the war.

Everyone in America had good reasons for joy, and few realized that the weapon that ended the war would shape the rest of our lives and those of our yet unborn children.

Open Wide

Have you been to the dentist lately? I have, and I'll have to admit that even though all the people in the dentist's office are great, I would just as soon remain at work.

Since I had to wait for my jaw to deaden after the fun shot from inside my jaw to my ear, I had time to contemplate the advances in dentistry made during my lifetime. I remember going to Dr. Phelps who had offices at the dime store on the south side of the square. His chair was similar to the barber chairs of today with the addition of a little white basin at the patient's left side for all the indelicate spitting and swishing. (Dr. Phelps' son later became Lieutenant Governor of Missouri, and I'm sure he had good teeth.)

Today, dentists have no little basin by the side of the reclining chair. Instead, I get a mouth full of vacuum cleaners, water fountains, cotton wedges, and C-clamps. With my feet higher than my head, the dentist can look down into my mouth without the neck-breaking position of former days. However, I began to feel like I was in a science fiction movie when the dentist and the assistant donned large plastic glasses, and he placed what looked like a radar gun in my mouth, pointed at the ailing tooth. I didn't get a chance to ask what this was for, since it's hard to talk with a gun, a vacuum cleaner, a water fountain, and two cotton wedges in my mouth. In fact, my dentist had the nerve to tell me he wished I would grow a bigger mouth. When I was able to talk, I informed him it was big enough for me to put my foot in quite often.

My dentist also told me he had not read any of my columns, and since I still have two return visits before I'm through with this procedure, I hope he doesn't start reading them this week!

One thing that Dr. Phelps and today's dentists have in common is the tendency to wait until your mouth is full of pounds of hardware to ask a question. Dr. Phelps always asked me when my father would be coming to town. Since I didn't know for sure anyway, I usually just shrugged my shoulders. That doesn't work too well today, as a mature person is supposed to know a few answers. I mumble an answer which dislodges the vacuum cleaner a bit so that it feels like it is sucking my cheek into its little tube.

Unlike my earlier visits with Dr. Phelps, who was a very good dentist for his time, I will have to admit that, except for the aforementioned inside-the-jaw shot, there is very little pain in current visits to the dentist. Like all medical practices these days, the worst pain comes when it is time to pay the bill.

Mom Bashing

Have you noticed how the media seems to be "mom bashing" these days? Comic strips depict moms of baby boomers as problems to overcome. An advertisement on television shows a mom waking up a grown son in the middle of the night, by telephone, because she can't get to sleep.

Another ad shows a young woman taking pain reliever because the headache, caused by Mom's visit, goes away quicker if she used a certain type type of pill. Then she does admit Mom suggested the medicine.

Situation comedies portray a visit from Mom as moments of adjustments and craziness that must be endured to placate the visitor. Most of the middle age-plus mothers who are continuing characters on the comedies are shown as eccentric, self-centered, demanding women. The young adult characters are deliriously happy when the folks, or Mom, plan to move away, and are devastated when the parents live close by.

Since I am a Mom, Grandmom, and Great-Grandmom, I hope this isn't the truth. I think back to my thirties and forties when we were raising our own children and remember only regrets when we were too far from home to see my parents often. We deliberately moved to be near them here in Vernon County and rejoiced that our three oldest children got to have a day-by-day relationship with their grandparents. I'm sure there were times when I scurried to hide a dirty dish or two or quickly make a bed when I saw my mother coming, but I don't remember ever wishing she wouldn't come.

Many adults quote their mom's advice from years past as the gospel truth. In *Forrest Gump*, Forrest quotes his deceased mother at every turn. Mom's advice is his standard to live by. But then Forrest is mentally retarded! I find myself reflecting on my mother's wisdom, realizing that I am now much older than she was when she gave me that insight. However, it doesn't diminish the value I put upon her teachings.

I wonder if this mom bashing is the follow-up of all the many years of mother-in-law jokes. Some of those are very cruel. Since eventually most mothers become mothers-in-law, also, we are now being hit with both barrels.

We're strong. We can take it, but to retaliate, I'd love to write a script that shows Mom as the heroine, and the ever-so-smart baby boomer child as the one who needs a patient guide out of problems.

If I had such a chance, I would entitle it, *Mom, Where Would You Be Without Her?*

That's Who I Am

Have you ever noticed that when we look at a picture of someone that was taken several years ago we usually laugh? Sometimes it is the clothes or hairstyle that strikes us as funny. But more often than not it is the actual physical appearance of the people photographed that amuses us. Most of us look better to our friends right now than we did in our old photos. I think many of us improve with age, just like fine wines (I am told).

Several of my older siblings are really outstanding looking in their eighties and nineties. I thought they looked great in their twenties and thirties, also, but when I look at the old pictures, I see that they are more attractive now. Maybe that is just a little sister's prejudice, but I notice this also in many of the old pictures we print in the paper or that I see on other people's living room walls.

The little birthday wishes put in the paper sometimes showing a gaped-tooth child who is now (heavens forbid) forty are intended to provoke a laugh at this aging person's expense. But we know that the fond parent who snapped that picture years ago thought the child was pretty cute then, too.

Maybe it boils down to the fact that we all look pretty good for the age we are right now. A toothless baby with drool coming out of the mouth is cute. A toothless older person with drool coming out of the mouth distresses us. But put in the teeth and wipe off the mouth and most of us look fairly good regardless of our age.

I sometimes change my mind when I watch a rerun of, for instance, *The Andy Griffith Show* and see the young, slim Andy Griffith walking along a road and then immediately see an aging, fat Andy Griffith plugging his newest records in a commercial. It is even worse when he seems to be walking along that same Mayberry road of his earlier years. And Opie with his freckled face and tousled hair is now occasionally seen with his bald head and maturing body. They certainly have each done well in the intervening years, but my earlier remark about us looking good at our age somehow doesn't hold up as well for some movie and television stars.

I thought Jimmy Stewart looked great even in his last years. He looked the same, only older. Henry Fonda was another who didn't change much in his mature years. But the recent pictures of the old captain of the *Love Boat* certainly wouldn't start many hearts pounding. Art Linkletter in the cameo appearances on the new *Kids Say The Darndest Things* looks very much the same as when he was host to the show years ago.

I wonder what makes the difference?

A change in weight and a big change in the amount of hair cause differences. Styles of hair and clothes create images that alter the total appearance. But I think the biggest factor is that we have a youthful image imprinted in our minds through years of seeing reruns of the old shows so that the sudden appearance of an aged person shocks us.

I have dozens of pictures on the walls in our home of loved ones at various ages. Each of them looks pretty great to me until I look at the one of me with long skinny legs twisted around each other in an awkward pose, my straight hair flying, and a shapeless dress hanging from my thin shoulders. I think I prefer a recent one of me with my ample chins, glasses, and wrinkles around the eyes.

Today I couldn't even twist my legs into that awkward position, and nothing has hung shapeless on me for years. I always want to snip off that one bunch of hair in the picture that hangs down below the rest, but generally, I feel fairly comfortable with who I am now. Those pictures of me in my youth showed a young person who not only looked but felt awkward. The years have taken that away from me, so now I only look fat and dumpy. But I don't mind.... That's who I am!

Fifty Years Is a Short Time Span

During the years, some events stand out as occasions where we vividly realize the passage of years. This awareness happened to me last week. My husband and I went to Columbia, Missouri, to attend our church's annual conference. We have been doing this each spring for thirty-five years. It is a great time to get together with old friends, make new ones, and remain involved in the church.

Many attending were seminary classmates and spouses of classmates of my husband. Others had served nearby churches or were on committees with one or the other of us. Years of working together formed bonds that we renew each year. However, this year I noticed a difference.

You probably think I'm going to comment how old our friends looked. Well, some did, but that was not the biggest change. What I noticed the most was that young kids were holding such responsible positions. Some of these youngsters had been ministers for only a few years—oh, maybe only twenty or so. They were in school when our gang was the group in responsible positions. Now they were the leaders. It's true some had turned gray or were bald, but to me they were young.

In past years when our friends got together over the dinner table or in lobbies, we made exciting plans. How we caucused in planning strategies to pass a resolution or get a certain person elected to an important position! We spent hours looking at possibilities to improve the ministry of the churches in the conference. We brainstormed new ideas.

But this year when we gathered, the conversation centered around cholesterol levels, exercise routines, gardening tips, the joys of grandchildren and great-grandchildren, and the pros and cons of retirement villages versus private homes. The same excitement shone in our eyes. The same anticipation animated our voices as we discussed these new topics. However, when break time was over, we each dutifully returned to assigned seats on the floor of the conference to remain responsible members of this governing body.

During one break, I drove by myself through the university city. I passed a teeming shopping mall on the spot where Lester and I lived at the end of World War II in an unused farmhouse out in the country. When we lived there, it was at least a half mile beyond the end of the bus line. Now the city extends several miles farther out. Places where we used to picnic in open country were suburban neighborhoods. All of this development happened in the fifty short years since we lived there.

These three incidents in my week showed me that I am *truly* middle age-plus when fifty years seems like a short time span!

College Tuition: $32.00 a Semester

Recently, I was eating with a group of friends who have just finished their college work or have children who enrolled in college. The subject of the cost of the different schools kept coming up. One person mentioned that a certain school only cost $12,000 a year including room and board.

I couldn't be quiet any longer. I asked the group if they knew what my college costs had been. Of course, they didn't, so I told them that the tuition and fees at the University of Missouri-Columbia were $32.00 a semester for a full academic load. My room and board was $32.00 a month in a girls' boarding house off campus. There was a silence until one friend asked, "But were you able to safely tie up your horse and buggy?"

Since my college years were also war years, a horse and buggy might have been a good deal as tires and gasoline were both rationed. But my sister and I did have an old Chevy coupe at school with us which we did not use very much because of the rationing. The only reason we had this luxury was that we used the car to move us and our stuff to Columbia from Washington, D.C., where our parents lived at the time.

After my parents moved to Washington, I was the first of the eight children to be allowed to go to college away from home. That happened only because Ellen was getting a second degree at Missouri after graduating from the University of Maryland. I don't know if it was out of concern for my sister that they let me go, or if it was my "tactful" argument that home sure wouldn't be fun anymore if I were the only kid still at home.

For whatever reason, I was permitted to accompany my sister to our home state university with the very reasonable in-state fees.

This decision altered my life as well as that of my sister. It was at Columbia that I met Lester, my future husband, who lived in a rooming house next door to the boarding house for girls. Since the boys at that house took their meals at our house, in spite of the war time shortage of men, we had a small friendly co-ed group for company. Several friendships began in those years, but I believe Lester and I were the only ones to marry. My sister finished her degree in two years, became what was then called a Home Demonstration Agent, and married a man in Laclede County where she was assigned.

These happenings show that there are no small decisions. Where we go to college, or where we are employed are not small decisions but may set the direction for our future. Where we choose to live, what friends we make, even whether we walk to class a certain route can lead to experiences that change our lives. This is exciting and somewhat scary, especially when we watch our children, grandchildren, or great-grandchildren make decisions or start hanging out with a certain group. But even we middle age-plus people experience changes because we were in the right or wrong place at the right or wrong time.

We hope that our years of wisdom will stand by us as we make small or big decisions each day, but I'm not sure that I do any better now than in the past. However, on the whole, I feel pretty good about most of my decisions along the way. I'm sure I got my money's worth with my $32.00 tuition cost and especially for the $32.00 room and board fee. I probably wouldn't be visiting with you from my own home town if Mrs. Chamberlain's Boarding House had not had an opening when we came to Columbia in 1944. I probably would be somewhere in the East not having half as much fun as I do with my irreverent friends who can joke with me about my age.